Developing Engineers and Technicians

Notes on giving guidance to engineers and technicians on how infrastructure can meet the needs of men and women

Brian Reed & Sue Coates

Water, Engineering and Development Centre
Loughborough University
2005

Water, Engineering and Development Centre
Loughborough University
Leicestershire
LE11 3TU UK

WEDC

Water, Engineering and Development Centre,
Loughborough University,
Leicestershire, LE11 3TU, UK

© WEDC, Loughborough University, 2005

Reed, B. J. and Coates, S. (2005)
Developing Engineers and Technicians –
Notes on giving advice on how infrastructure can meet the needs of men and women

A reference copy of this publication is also available online from:
http://www.lboro.ac.uk/wedc/

ISBN 13 Paperback: 9781843801108
ISBN Library Ebook: 9781788532907
Book DOI: http://dx.doi.org/10.3362/9781788532907

A catalogue record for this book is available from the British Library.

WEDC (The Water, Engineering and Development Centre) at Loughborough University in the UK is one of the world's leading institutions concerned with education, training, research and consultancy for the planning, provision and management of physical infrastructure for development in low- and middleincome countries.

This document is an output from a project funded by the UK
Department for International Development (DFID)
for the benefit of low-income countries.
The views expressed are not necessarily those of DFID.

Designed and produced at WEDC
by Sue Plummer

This edition is reprinted and distributed by Practical Action Publishing.
Since 1974, Practical Action Publishing has published and disseminated books and information in support of international development work throughout the world. Practical Action Publishing trades only in support of its parent charity objectives and any profits are covenanted back to Practical Action (Charity Reg. No. 247257, Group VAT Registration No. 880 9924 76).

Acknowledgements

These training notes where produced by a project team consisting of Sue Coates, Marie Fry, and Brian Reed, led by Ian Smout. The team wishes to thank the following people for their assistance in preparing this publication.

The project was advised by an international review group, consisting of:

- Peter Sinclair
- Ben Fawcett
- John Collett
- Alison Barrett
- Dr Morag Bell
- Lizette Burgers
- Brendan A Doyle
- Louiza Duncker

- Renu Gera
- Martin Gillham
- Sarah House
- Margaret Ince
- Cyrus Njiru
- Archana Patkar
- Rupert Talbot
- Ilse Wilson

These people reviewed drafts of the guidelines and the final draft was also peer reviewed in detail by the UK Department for International Development (DFID). Special mention is made of Sarah House's contribution in laying the foundations for this project. Thanks must also go to the students and staff members of WEDC and Loughborough University who contributed material and comments for the project, especially: Paul Deverill, Julie Fisher, Margaret Ince, Hazel Jones, Rose Lidonde, Cyrus Njiru, Rebecca Scott, Brian Skinner, Mike Smith, Maria Ximena Guavita and Ngozi Nora Ishiekwene

The research and development of this book and the associated training material was assisted by the following partner organisations:

- Mvula Trust (South Africa)
- CSIR (South Africa)
- UNICEF (India)

Together with other valuable contributions including by staff from UNICEF (Nigeria), WaterAid (Zambia) and Médecins sans Frontières.

Brian Reed, Editor

Contents

Units

Checklists

Suggested modules

Introduction

Why these notes are needed

These notes are to help develop awareness amongst engineers in low-income countries of why the needs of men and women should be considered in development projects and how they, as technical professionals, can meet those needs. The trainer/facilitator/project manager should adapt these units to suit the needs of the audience, based on their current level of awareness and knowledge of issues such as social exclusion, gender and the engineering response.

Who these notes are for

Technical staff need to continuously develop their competency if they are going to provide a professional service. This builds on their initial training and provides new skills suited to the work they are carrying out. By basing learning in the context of their job, the process is relevant and can be applied readily. Learning does not just involve gaining new skills such as computer proficiency or management techniques, but also changing values and attitudes, such as customer care or environmental awareness. These notes are designed to support the training of engineers and technicians in developing an awareness of gender issues. They can be used at any level from trainee to project manager.

The trainer can be one of a variety of people. The manager of a team can use the notes in a variety of situations at work. They can be used by trainers carrying out other professional development activities, such as instruction on contracts or technical subjects.

The notes have been designed for people who would normally either manage engineering projects, run engineering courses or chair engineering meetings. They are not a standard "gender" training pack. The person leading the units should have an understanding of the participants' background, priorities and concerns. Many gender trainers are women; a man leading the units can break the image that gender issues are for women, making them more relevant to the largely male engineering audience. This will also help break down one stereotype; just because an engineer is female, this does not necessarily mean that she knows any more about gender issues in development contexts than a male engineer.

How these notes are presented

There are over 30 separate units and seven checklists for progress meetings. These can be used as single activities or as part of a series of units.

Engineers and scientists are often linear thinkers, where one idea leads on to another. The suggested modules take the group through various stages to raise awareness and provide examples. Whereas college students will take in information, often with no context to relate it to, more experienced staff will be able to draw on their existing knowledge and relate what they are learning to their own experience. Often "learning by doing" will allow the participants to experience the issue under discussion, rather than hear about it in a passive fashion that is unrelated to their own knowledge.

There are three stages to getting the key messages across:

■ Raising awareness that men and women have different roles and needs, and that this is relevant to engineers (units 1 to unit 6).

■ Showing how these roles and needs can be identified (units 6 to 12).

■ Responding to these issues as engineers in daily work, both in terms of:

- design/construction/operation (units 12 to 23).and

- engineering organization (project, department or company) (units 24 to 32).

After the individual units, there are a series of checklists. These can be used to put what is learnt in these units into action, by including the list of points in progress meetings and reports. They should be integrated into standard work patterns, rather than as a separate activity.

Although these notes have been developed with the assistance of a variety of engineering and project management staff, your situation is unique. At the end of the training notes are a series of suggested training modules. These groups of units are given to provide inspiration, but you will need to adapt them to suit your training style and the level of interest of your audience.

Visual aids have been kept to a minimum, so these units can be followed in the field, on site or office where people work. This means that a specific training course need not be conducted. The training should, as far as is possible be seen as part of everyday work and not as a separate activity which can be bolted on to engineers' normal roles. Where visual aids are needed, only outlines are given. These will need to be re-drawn for your own context and using the materials available locally.

The units and checklists can be used in a number of ways

■ Individual staff development tools (used as single units within the work environment)

■ In service training:

- Stand alone units

- As part of a broader training programme (e.g. technical or managerial)

- As a series of sessions over several weeks (e.g. at lunchtimes, as an extension to project meetings)

- As a concise course on involving men and women in infrastructure development

■ Meeting agendas

■ Practical application in the field - especially in developing participatory methods

Discussions

The aim of many of the units is to get people to think about a subject and if necessary, change their outlook. Rather than telling them what they should think, the facilitator should encourage debate and discussion. Many of the units are based on a led discussion on one topic. Suggested questions are marked and some possible responses included.

? Is there a "correct" answer to all of the questions? (no, the responses will vary with the context).

Next to each unit is a set of points for the trainer. These short summaries are to help plan sessions and give the main purpose of the session, the gender and engineering messages and an approximate duration. The purpose may be to develop awareness, change perceptions, teach a particular skill or transfer knowledge.

The main part of the unit contains a possible procedure, with sample questions and discussion points, background material and hints and suggestions.

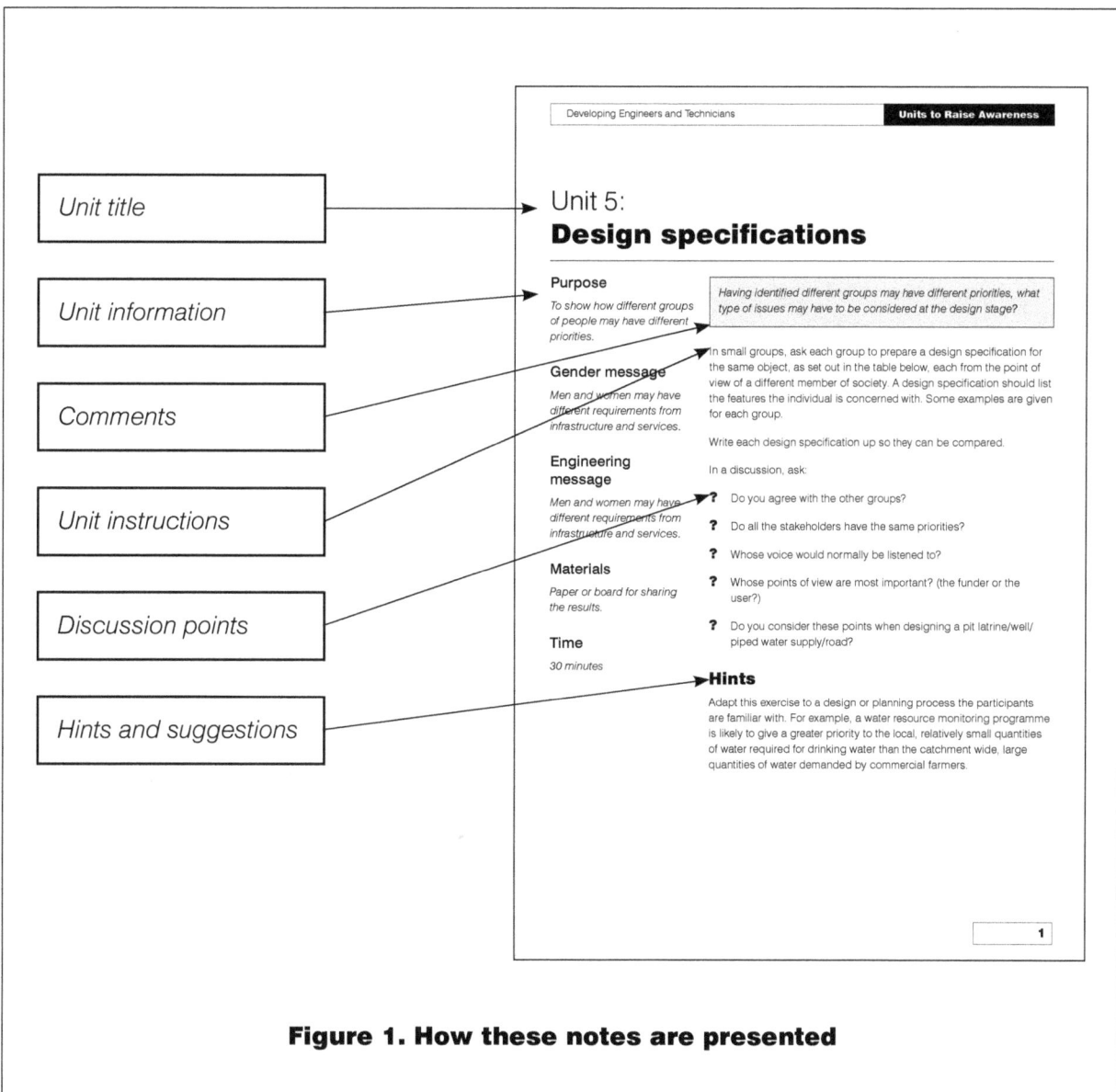

Figure 1. How these notes are presented

How you can make the most of these notes

Deciding upon a course title

In developing these notes, it was found that engineers did not readily attend training on "gender". The course title (if one is needed) should concentrate on engineers and make it valuable to their work, such as "The engineer and society" or "Infrastructure for all".

Learning style and participation

Engineers deal in knowledge and skills. Sociologists deal with values and awareness. Using concrete examples and case studies allows ideas to be illustrated rather than conceptualised in an abstract fashion. In raising awareness of socially excluded people, such as women, engineers will have to recognise that there is a value in the exercise, personally, professionally and for the communities concerned. Engineers also normally learn in a logical sequence, so the order of the training is important.

Participants are not "taught" gender, but have to develop an understanding and acceptance of the issues. This is why the sessions have opportunities for discussion rather than lecturing. Ensure that one group (e.g. senior/ male/ older staff) does not dominate the discussion, but also do not force people to take part if they feel uncomfortable in voicing their opinions in the full group. The use of smaller groups, which can be varied throughout the sessions, can help people to contribute. Criticism (by the trainer or other participants) stops people talking freely and so should be handled carefully. The trainer is not trying to teach from a position of superior knowledge, but to help the participants find out for themselves. Be aware of conflict, as the facilitator may be seen as different (e.g. professional or field staff, managers or staff, expatriate or local, outsider or local, black or white, female or male) and imposing external values on the group.

Language

> Engineers can be wary of "gender issues". The language used and the way the issue is presented can prove to be a barrier. Often "gender" is imposed on a project, without any acceptance by the project officers or acceptance that it is relevant to the engineering product. However, meeting the needs of all members of society is a core objective of engineering. Do not obscure the central message with unnecessary jargon. Make the sessions enjoyable - many of the messages are not conveying factual information but persuading engineers to be more aware of people who are often ignored in the engineering process.

Do not push the "gender" aspect too much at the start of the session. People need to decide for themselves that it is important. In some disciplines or areas, ethnicity or class may be a more important indicator of exclusion.

Base the sessions on your own (personal or organizational) experience but always position your messages so that the individuals in the group can engage. The sessions need to start by relating to issues that engineers are familiar with, rather than external priorities. Engineers are more likely to respond to issues such as the increased efficiency and effectiveness of projects due to involvement of all of society, rather than abstract ideas of rights. They do need to be aware however that rights are an important component of why inclusion is being promoted.

Support

Reading the companion book, *Infrastructure for All* is strongly recommended. The guidelines go into more detail about the subject and will provide the trainer with a firm foundation to get the message across. This will also help answer some of the questions that may be asked.

There are a series of case studies to support these units. They can be used as additional study material or illustrations of specific issues. They are from many different countries and often are based on cultural factors, but this is not necessarily the important issue in this context. Concentrate on the engineering problem; if the particular cultural problem does not occur in your area, there will probably be a similar issue that you can use to illustrate the same point. For example, the problem of a woman who is wearing a sari being able to access a water tank by climbing a ladder without potential injury or compromise is mirrored in many other countries where women wear long skirts or other sorts of restrictive clothing.

Many of the units are based on participatory assessments often used on community projects. These have been adapted for engineers and made shorter to fit in with the timetable of the units. For more information, there are books and guidelines on these activities, for example *Methodology for Participatory Assessments with Communities, Institutions and Policy Makers* (Dayal, van Wijk and Mukherjee, Water and Sanitation Programme).

Timing

Timings may vary. For example, if you have four participative units, one after the other, each may last 30 minutes so the total time is two hours. If you split into four groups, it may take 10 minutes to organize the groups, but then the bulk of the unit takes part at the same time, for about 20 minutes. Report back then takes 10 minutes each, a total of 70 minutes. More groups will extend the feedback period. Do try to start and finish on time and do not forget to allow for tea breaks.

The timings given are only for the training of engineers. If some of the participative units were being carried out with a community, then the 30 minutes to demonstrate a problem tree may become three hours, allowing for people to become familiar with the exercise and discuss the issues at their own pace.

Visual aids and handouts

Many of the units are visual. Many were developed as part of community appraisal projects and had to allow for people who were illiterate or did not have the ability to express themselves in writing. Some of the information cannot be easily written down, such as maps. The use of diagrams, charts should appeal to engineers, as they are used to using these and symbols to represent issues under discussion.

There are no handouts, as these notes are designed for use in a variety of situations, without access to overhead projectors or photocopiers. A ten-page booklet has been prepared to introduce engineers to some of the topics discussed. This booklet and the case studies included in this pack can also be downloaded from the WEDC Website: (http://www.lboro.ac.uk/wedc/projects/msgender/index.htm).

Getting the message across

Before you start a training session, you need to prepare the area. Normally engineering training involves one person standing at the front of the class and instructing the class. This is good for transferring knowledge and factual information, but may not be so good when you are trying to develop people's values and explain concepts. Rather than sit in rows, it may be better to have a less formal layout, such as a circle of chairs or at least a curve. Decide what you and the participants will be comfortable with. Many of these units involve working in small groups or having a general discussion with everybody, so it is useful if the whole group can see each other. Rather than just passively receiving information, the people should be involved in the units, hence the term "participants" rather than course attendees.

The location could be a training room. As these units do not require any particular equipment, they could equally be carried out in an office or on site.

Besides making the learning area comfortable, the participants should be relaxed and open to debate. There may be social barriers to free discussion, such as not wanting to contradict a senior staff member, or women not wanting to confront men's values. Sometimes it is better to have separate groups; at other times, the groups need to have their assumptions challenged. There are various ways to break down some of the barriers at the start of a session. The simplest is for participants to introduce themselves and perhaps give a bit of background - perhaps unrelated to their jobs so they are recognised as individuals rather than a "design engineer" or "technician". One piece of information could be factual (e.g. home place), whilst another could be subjective (e.g. favourite food). The people leading the unit should also introduce themselves. Again, ask questions that do not challenge the participants' values too much at the start.

Jargon

Although the use of specialist terms has been kept to a minimum, some social scientist language is used. This is because each term has a specific meaning. Understanding some of these terms will make communication between engineers and social scientist easier.

Gender: *This relates to social relationships between men and women, as opposed to the physical differences (termed sex). This term is often misused - care should be taken to say "women" when women are specifically being discussed and "gender" when social issues concerning men and women are discussed.*

Socio-economic: *Socio-economic issues include a variety of specific factors, such as wealth, culture, religion or employment. It is a general term summarising all these aspects. An engineering parallel would be, say, structural engineering, which encompasses material science, mechanics, dynamics, economics, aesthetics and construction safety.*

Empowerment: *The long term change in social status resulting from a socially weak group increasing their power, possibly by dominant people relinquishing power, coupled with the weaker group gaining the skills and resources to take on the responsibilities.*

How you can use the units

In-service training

The units can be used as single activities (e.g. at a lunchtime or associated with a general staff meeting) or combined to form modules. A group of several units could be included with other training activities (e.g., a course on sanitation could have a proportion of the time devoted to gender sensitive design). Alternatively, several units could be grouped together to form modules. Four modules are suggested at the end of this introduction. These could be used as a full course, but preferably could be used over a period of time (e.g. lunchtimes or one afternoon a week), so they are fully integrated into current work patterns.

Project meetings

Continuing professional development does not only take place in formal training situations. Opportunities for developing your staff can occur during meetings. A series of checklists are included. These can be used at different times in the project cycle or for different types of infrastructure. They can be used to set an agenda for progress meetings or provide a format for a review at the end of each project stage. They are written as a series of queries and often can be followed by a supplementary question regarding any differences between the answer for men or women.

Field use

These notes have not been designed for direct use in the field. However they can be adapted and used in conjunction with other more comprehensive publications on participation (e.g. Methodology for Participatory Assessments, Dayal, van Wijk and Mukherjee IRC/Water and Sanitation Program, or Participatory Ranking, Experiences, Perceptions and Partnership (PREPP) - a tool for engineer's to engage with communities (Coates et al, WEDC 2004). Units will take longer and will need to be explained to the participants. If the engineer is working with a social scientist, then these units can provide inspiration so the social scientist can examine technical as well as social and economic information.

Adapting the material

This material has been prepared mainly for water and sanitation engineers. It can be adapted for other groups of technical staff. Many of the units are not specific to water supply or sanitation. Those that are can be adapted, either for other sectors or more specific groups.

As an example, if the participants are all working in water resource management, Unit 1 - Defining civil engineering, could be altered to defining Integrated Water Resource Management and Unit 5 - Design specifications could be adapted to looking at a water resource monitoring programme, rather than a pit latrine design.

Frequently asked questions

> *These training notes have been developed to give engineers and technical staff a greater awareness of gender issues and how they, as engineers can respond to them. Engineering professional development has traditionally been about knowledge, whilst social science works with concepts and values.*

There is often a resistance to "gender" as engineers feel that an external set of values is being imposed on them. The following questions are often posed.

? 'It's an unfair focus on women. What about the needs of men?'

- Women do have different physical and social needs from men and these need to be given a higher priority than they have in the past. Men's needs have been established as normal practice.

- Men do also have specific needs, consider violence from war, risk of HIV/AIDS or commercial as opposed to domestic work. These are issues for both men and women, but have different patterns, causes and outcomes.

- Men have pressures to conform. Macho cultures or pressure not to be seen to be "weak" can constrain the way men behave.

- Women are often ignored as their voice is not heard at a decision-making level and so they do need to be explicitly involved.

- Just working with women will not rectify exclusion. Keeping women's issues separate and not part of core development activities will not change inequitable practices. Both men and women need to be considered together.

- With any socially excluded group, the dominant party (e.g. rich men) is just as much part of the problem as any excluded group (e.g. poor women). The excluded group need to be given the skills and opportunities to participate whilst the powerful group need to be persuaded to include the more vulnerable members of society - for the benefit of all.

- "Gender" does not mean "women" (although sometimes it is used in the wrong context). It is a technical term used by social scientists to describe the sociological differences and relationships between women and men.

- If you do not like the word "gender" or your audience does not like it (because of preconceptions, language difficulties or educational background), there are alternatives. You could use "women" or "men and women" when talking about specific groups of people. More general terms such as use "socially excluded", "social diversity", "vulnerable", "unequal influence", "marginalized" or another socio-economic measure that they may be more familiar with, such as "poor" or "landless".

? 'It's not about gender, it's about culture/religion/rich and poor'

- Engineers are used to using many measurements and parameters. For example, pipes are characterised by material (plastic, concrete, etc.), wall thickness, diameter, pressure rating and cost. Normally only one or two key indicators are used to describe a pipe - for example a 100-mm ductile iron pipe. Societies are much more variable than a simple pipe and so many more parameters are needed. However, to start any analysis there are a few key indicators, the most common being gender and wealth. Looking at these two measures will give a good insight into the social structure of a community.

- Many socio-economic parameters are linked. Thus social differences between men and women may be due to cultural or religious practices, but in every society, there is a difference between the roles of men and women. In terms of a practical impact, these variations in role are easier to identify and address than the cultural background.

- Gender and poverty are very closely linked. A greater proportion of poor people are women rather than men. If a man is poor then his wife and young children are likely to be poorer. If you want to reduce poverty, then it will be more efficient to target the majority of poor people (women) rather than a more vocal minority.

? 'Gender is not an issue that engineers should be concerned with'

- Deliberately ignoring the differing needs and perceptions of social groups on the grounds of lack of time, cultural sensitivity or sectoral limits is not a valid argument.

- Engineers do change cultural and religious practices, by their work and example. This can be direct or indirect, planned or incidental. They should be aware of this and ensure they are not making life more difficult for certain members of society.

- Engineering infrastructure is for the whole of society and should not exclude half of the population.

- Past engineering practice has dealt with gender, but often negatively by excluding women. Consciously or inadvertently, technical issues impact on men and women differently.

? 'It's western feminist ideals being put on non-western societies and promoting women's equality constitutes undue interference in the a country's internal affairs'

- Men and women have different roles in all societies. Women nearly always have a lower social and economic status.

- Responses to social inequalities do need to be specific to the context. Western feminist ideas were developed in response to a particular set of inequalities.

- Deliberately setting out to change society, culture or religion is the subject of ethics. Should you impose your view on others because you think one group is oppressed? What right do you have to change cultural practices and are you going to support vulnerable people during the whole of the period of social change - which may be many years?

- Change happens from within. A strident campaign puts socially dominant groups on the defensive, rather than working with all members of society. Local men and women have to work together to see what they want to change and set their own priorities.

? 'Gender issues are also about human rights?'

- Development programmes can take a variety of approaches. Some are rights based, others are socially driven or have an economic goal, some are environmental or have a religious dimension. Often the project may be described using this primary goal, but will have other incidental impacts.

- Gender is a component of all these approaches and valid reasons for focussing on the needs of men and women can be assigned to any of the approaches.

? 'Why is it nearly always women that work on researching, teaching and advancing gender issues?'

- Gender studies grew out of women's studies, which naturally attracted largely female participation

- The people most concerned with socially excluded groups are likely to be those who identify most closely to that group, thus women are more likely to champion the cause of other women. This is important in trying to promote a message. Enabling men to relate to discrimination against women by comparing it to any racial, financial or class issues they are aware of is one way of raising awareness.

- The same question could be turned around - why is it always men who are engineers? Many societies still seem to encourage men into engineering and women into social sciences. This is also directly linked to which sex has best access to education and lifelong learning opportunities.

- Although there are not many men working on gender issues in infrastructure development contexts, those that do are significant as it shows that gender is not just a "woman's issue". Where possible select a man to work with men on raising gender awareness, an engineer to work with engineers. This reduces some of the suspicion that some men have about the subject.

- Just because an engineer is female, it does not mean that she knows anything about gender in the context of infrastructure development and engineering. She will at least have had the same undergraduate engineering training as her male colleagues.

Unit 1:
Defining civil engineering

Purpose

To focus on the role of engineers and their relationship with society.

To broaden the focus of engineering, considering social, economic and environmental implications.

Gender message

Information has an impact on society

Engineering message

Engineering is for society and society includes everyone.

Materials

Paper and pens

Time

20 minutes

? Ask the whole group for some examples of the results of civil engineering (e.g. dams, roads, buildings, pipelines, water supplies, drains, railways, bridges)

Break into small groups (e.g. 4 people) and ask each group to come up with a definition of civil engineering. Once they are ready, these should be written up so everybody can see them. Ask the group for comments on each other's suggestions.

Write up the following definition

Engineering is ...

The art of directing the great sources of power in Nature for the use and convenience of man

Thomas Tredgold (1788 - 1829)

Alternatives for this definition have often been suggested, but it does show two aspects. The technical side **"art of directing the great sources of power in Nature"** *and the social side* **"for the use and convenience of man"**. *This second aspect is not always obvious from the list of infrastructure given at the start of the exercise.*

Ask the whole group what the aims of civil engineering are - not *what* we produce but *why*? Ideas might include:

? To improve economic performance of an area

? To protect the environment

? To make people's lives better

? For political gestures

? To improve health

*The word **civil** in civil engineering is related to the word **citizen**. Thus civil engineering is engineering for citizens rather than any other (e.g. military, industrial) purpose. If there is time, discuss the benefits of public and private infrastructure (e.g. toll roads and bridges, private water supplies).*

Infrastructure is public because the costs and benefits can be shared *efficiently* and *equitably*.

Hints

Read chapter one of the Guidance book.

Check whether any of the participants pick up on the use of "man" in Tredgold's definition?

For groups with a more specific focus, ask the participants to define their field (e.g. water resources or railways) and the reasons for capital investment in that field.

Unit 2:
Who makes up society?

Purpose

To show that although everybody is an individual, they can share characteristics with a group of people.

Gender message

Somebody's gender is a good indicator of his or her social status.

Engineering message

None

Materials

Paper or blackboard

Time

20 minutes

---

*If engineering is for the **"use and convenience of society"** - who is society? Sociologists study societies and in the early development of the subject they adopted a "scientific" approach. This assumed that society was made up of defined groups and you could define somebody by the groups they belong to.*

Think of some groups in society and draw a Venn diagram to illustrate this. (Figure 2). (Note: more rich men than rich women - or more poor women than poor men). Some of these differences are physical (e.g. age) and some are socio-economic (e.g. rich/poor). The divide between men and women is both physical (sex) and social (known as gender).

? Does membership of any particular group determine your place in society?

? What are the physical differences between men and women? (strength(?), size, child birth, menstruation, physical appearance)

? What are the social differences (e.g. education access, social status, wealth, legal status, membership of government, religious status and job allocation).

? Is this approach true - are your individual characteristics more important than the general characteristics you share with other people?

If you are a rich, single, healthy, (etc.) man, then you are in a group all by yourself. Another way of analysing society is to consider that individuals determine how a society works, rather than the control of social groups.

Allow the participants time to debate the two viewpoints, to decide the strengths and weakness of each approach. Modern thinking blends the two schools of thought, so people's actions and where they are in the structure of society determines how society works.

? If you wanted to make a rapid assessment of any society, which of these various parameters would you look at first?

? If you have a particular project (e.g. education or health), then age or health may be important

? If a society has rigid divisions (class or caste), these may appear to dominate the society

? Gender is easy to identify

In any society, wealth and gender are very significant indicators of social status.

Hints

Use groups that the participants can relate to e.g. alumni of universities (social) or height (physical). Emphasise diversity.

Example of a Venn diagram[1] of society

An alternative approach would get people to physically stand in groups around the room and slowly introduce more categories; eventually each participant will be in a group by themselves.

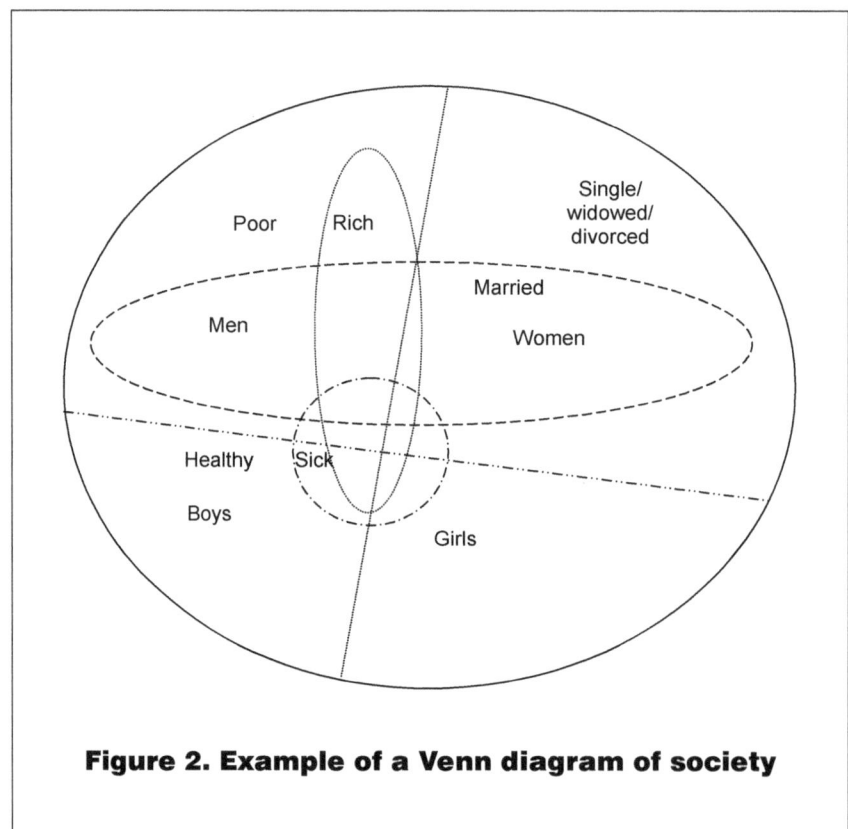

Figure 2. Example of a Venn diagram of society

---

[1] Venn diagrams are sometimes locally called 'chapatti' diagrams.

Unit 3:
Social exclusion

Purpose

To find out what the best indicators of social exclusion are.

Gender message

Gender is a good indicator of social exclusion.

Engineering message

Other disciplines have their own indicators for measuring significant features.

Other disciplines have their own jargon - but then so does engineering.

Materials

None

Time

20 minutes

Following the Unit on *"who makes up society"*, we know that people belong to a variety of groups.

? Who has the greatest social status - and who has the least?

? Which people have the most influence over decision-making? (rich, educated, certain ethic groups, men, etc.)

? Who has the least influence over decision-making? (poor, lesser or uneducated, certain ethic groups, women, disabled etc.)

The second group is sometimes referred to as "socially excluded", "vulnerable" or "disenfranchised".

? What are the easiest ways to identify these people?

Simple indicators of social exclusion are economic ("the poor") and social (class, sex, caste, tribe). This latter group will vary from context to context. However, the social position of women relative to men is nearly always lower. Some women will have influence in some cases, but these are likely to be rich, educated and well connected. Starting a sociological analysis by looking at the poor and women is the most efficient way of identifying the majority of people normally excluded from decision making. Poverty and sex are often related, there being more poor women than poor men (e.g. widows, lesser or uneducated women, women without the vote, women without property or decision making rights).

Gender as an indicator of social exclusion

? Ask the group if they understand the word "gender"?

> *This word is a technical word and often misunderstood. It does not mean "women".*

The social differences and relationships between men and women are termed "gender". This is a technical term. If the group speak more than one language, ask them to translate it into another language. It is likely that the word, or concept does not translate very easily and often the nearest is "sex". This will require some discussion to come a mutual understanding of the term. However it is mutually described, it is usually the case that women have a lower social status than men.

?   What are the problems with a low social status?

Generally, lower access to education, justice, political representation/ decision-making, resources (land, credit) and healthcare. People with a low social status are less "visible" and so public facilities often ignore their needs, limiting their opportunities for self-improvement.

?   As another thought, did anybody mention children?

Hints

One of the problems is the use of technical language. Use some engineering terms to demonstrate how people from one sector may be misunderstood (e.g. stress, strain, sewer, sewerage, sewage). If you have people from different disciplines, ask one group to explain a complex issues to the others - without specialist terms.

Unit 4:
Social inclusion

Purpose

To find out how engineers can meet the needs of the socially excluded.

Gender message

Gender inequities can be addressed by strategic and practical responses.

Engineering message

Engineers can address social exclusion by practical and strategic actions.

Materials

None

Time

20 minutes

Social exclusion is a social problem so needs a social solution. How can this be addressed?

- By improving their social status (giving them the confidence to take part in society and encouraging society to include them). This is long term[2].

- The dominant group has to allow the excluded group to take part in decision-making. They have to realise that the poor/women do have a role and have their own priorities.

- The excluded group also needs the courage and ability to voice their own concerns[3].

- If one group gains influence, will other groups lose power, or does everybody gain? Think of a variety of examples (kings and democracy, specialists and popular opinion).

This type of social change takes a long time.

As engineers, there is normally neither the time nor the resources on an infrastructure project to address these social issues directly. However, engineers can ensure that their actions do not reinforce local prejudice.

- Through equitable employment and decision-making.

- By improving their access to resources (education, legal status, physical resources).

- Engineers can design the infrastructure to be pro-poor or pro-women. Women spend a long time collecting water, so ensure that water delivery where the women want it is given priority. The poor do not drive cars, so roads should be designed for pedestrians and public transport as well as lorries.

- Ensure that the engineer's organization practises what it preaches - are there any barriers to any group of society working in your organization?

These actions can be medium or even short term and *practical*. This

---

[2] Sometimes called *strategic*.

[3] Sociologists call this *empowerment*.

may be considered just concerned with the welfare of the socially excluded rather than their social status. If the infrastructure is to meet the needs of these people, then the designs have to be discussed with them to find out what their needs are. The excluded need the skills and opportunities to make their voice heard, so there is an element of empowerment.

In developing responses to gender inequalities, social actions have been promoted as important. Practical actions have not been given the same priority as they may be considered as a welfare response, treating women as passive beneficiaries rather than being actively involved. Engineers can take the lead on this area, involving men and women in the development of their own infrastructure, meeting their basic needs and priorities.

Unit 5:
Design specifications

Purpose

To show how different groups of people may have different priorities.

Gender message

Men and women may have different requirements from infrastructure and services.

Engineering message

Men and women may have different requirements from infrastructure and services.

Materials

Paper or board for sharing the results.

Time

30 minutes

Having identified different groups may have different priorities, what type of issues may have to be considered at the design stage?

In small groups, ask each group to prepare a design specification for the same object, as set out in the table below, each from the point of view of a different member of society. A design specification should list the features the individual is concerned with. Some examples are given for each group.

Write each design specification up so they can be compared.

In a discussion, ask:

?   Do you agree with the other groups?

?   Do all the stakeholders have the same priorities?

?   Whose voice would normally be listened to?

?   Whose points of view are most important? (the funder or the user?)

?   Do you consider these points when designing a pit latrine/well/ piped water supply/road?

Hints

Adapt this exercise to a design or planning process the participants are familiar with. For example, a water resource monitoring programme is likely to give a greater priority to the local, relatively small quantities of water required for drinking water than the catchment wide, large quantities of water demanded by commercial farmers.

Table 1: Suggested examples of infrastructure and people with a stake in the design					
Item	Group 1	Group 2	Group 3	Group 4	Group 5
Pit latrine	World Health Organisation official (hand washing facilities, number of latrines, programme)	Builder (amount of materials, time of year/weather, dimensions, programme, number of users)	Woman with baby (size of door, light, easy to clean slab, handrail, flies, smell, privacy, safety, water, location)	Community leader (long lasting, status, cost, acceptability by the community, safe)	Groundwater specialist (depth, location of water sources, groundwater contamination
Hand dug well	Woman (location, height of wall, queuing time, lifting device)	Community leader (long lasting, status, cost)	Builder (amount of materials, time of year/weather, dimensions, programme)	Water vendor (queuing time, water lifting device)	Landowner (water rights, use of water - cattle, domestic, washing, ownership)
Piped water supply	Builder (Labour required, programme, design, availability of materials)	Woman (operating cost, location of taps, other facilities - washing, taste, availability)	Water resource planner (Water required, water available, financial viability)	Environmentalist (construction impact, long-term impact, pollution, resource depletion)	Water vendor (work opportunities)
Water resource monitoring plan	Commercial sugar cane farmer (Cost of water, availability, timing)	Hydrologist (Data, accuracy, ease of collection, representative)	Health worker (Water purity, droughts, floods)	Environmentalist (Pollution, erosion)	Village woman (water reliability, water location, water purity, floods)
Road	Government official (cost, sustainability, programme, economic development, social impact)	Builder (not too much cut and fill, materials, programme)	Lorry driver (direct, fast, smooth, stopping places)	Village woman (buses, links to local villages, access to markets, increased food security, pedestrian access)	Village elder (road safety - traffic accidents, economic impact)

Unit 6:
Institutional analysis

Purpose

To show that people belong to different groups and these groups may be influenced by factors such as gender or employment.

Gender message

Men and women may belong to different groups.

Engineering message

Engineers may belong to different groups to people who are not engineers.

Materials

Paper and pens, flip chart or black/white board.

Time

30 minutes

Use a Venn diagram to show how society can be divided into groups.

> *Groups or institutions play an important part of how society works. One way of analysing a society is to look at how institutions relate to each other.*

? List organizations that at least one participant belongs to. These do not have to be formal bodies, but could just be a regular user (e.g. cinema), for example:

- professional bodies/institutions/unions

- social clubs (e.g. sports)

- religious groups

- political/democratic groups (parties, councils)

- financial (savings/bank)

> *Some people may be member of several groups, but is there a pattern? A Venn diagram showing the membership of every body may get complicated and not bring out simple relationships (see example). An alternative is to arrange the groups according to simple criteria. This can be shown on a flip chart, black/whiteboard or using pieces of paper. Two examples shown; one for groups and their relationships with the engineering organization and another for a gender analysis.*

This unit shows the membership of groups, but does not show if groups are exclusive, why they are exclusive or how to make them inclusive. This would require more detailed investigation.

Hints

Compare the groups engineers belong to as engineers and the variation according to gender - are engineering organizations all "male"?

Member of group 2

Member of group 1

Member of groups 2, 3 & 4

Member of group 3

Member of groups 3 & 4

Venn diagram

Only people within the
organization are members of
this group

The organization
boundaries

Some people are members of one
or both of these groups

Everybody in the organization
is a member of this group

Groups and the organization

Group of men
only

Group of both men
and women

Group of mainly
women

Divide between men and
women

Groups and gender

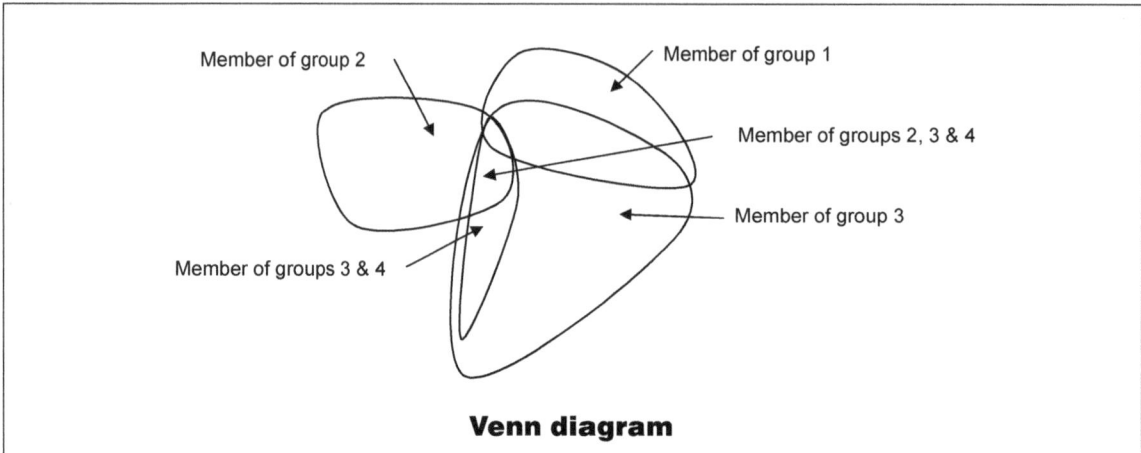

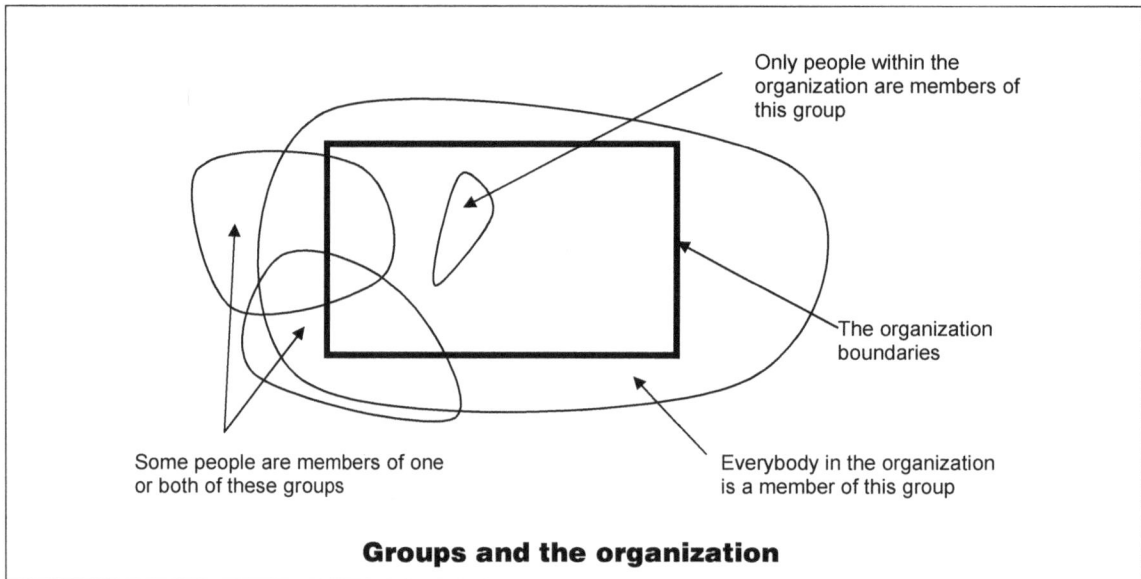

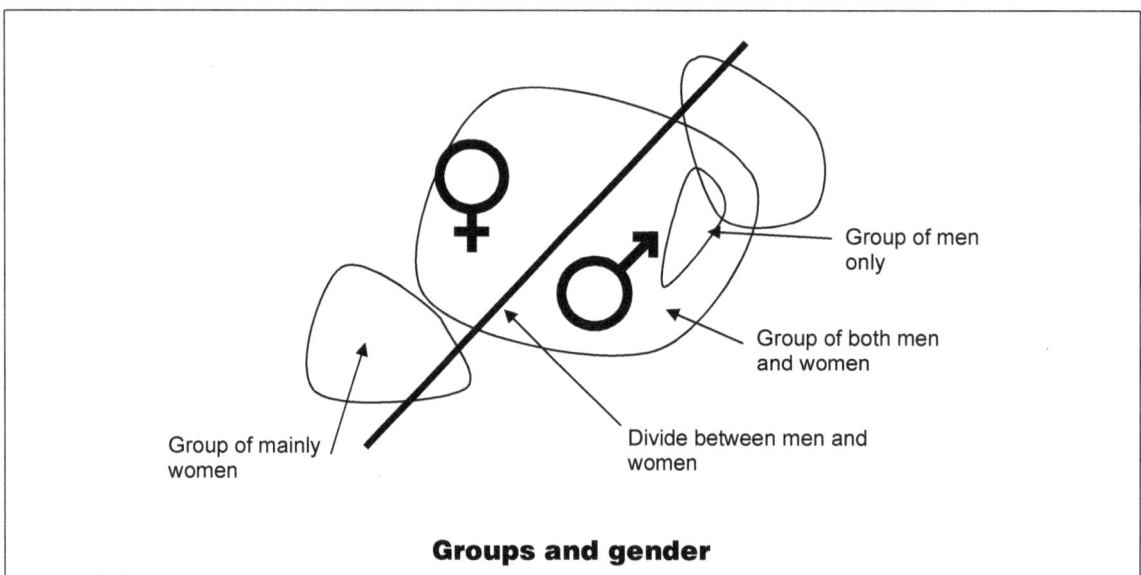

Figure 3. Examples of institutional analysis

Unit 7:
What do you do with your time?

Purpose

To show that men and women may use their time differently.

Gender message

Men and women do different work; women do more domestic work, men do more paid work, their community work has different status.

Consultation should be planned for a time when the whole community can attend.

Engineering message

Infrastructure has a variety of purposes. Commercial uses may be valued financially, but other uses have non-monetary value.

Materials

Large sheets of paper and pens (or similar).

Time

30 minutes

Either (A)

In small groups (e.g. 4 people), perhaps divided according to age, sex, seniority, job, etc. ask each group to draw up a diagram showing how a typical member of the group spends their time during the day (see example).

Or (B)

In small groups (e.g. 4 people), perhaps divided according to age, sex, seniority, job, etc. ask each group to draw up a diagram showing how a typical member of the group spends their time during the year (see example).

In a general discussion, ask:

? Could you provide the information for a "typical" member? How representative is it?

? Are there any variations between different groups?

? What information does this provide other participants (e.g. everybody is different, there may be similarities within groups, but differences with other groups).

? What information does this provide project managers (e.g. differences between social groups, when to hold meetings)

? What information does this provide engineers? (e.g. when to carry out construction), how long certain activities take (e.g. washing clothes)

? Does it raise the awareness of socio-economic issues?

If this was being carried out by a low income community:

? What types of work would be recorded? (domestic (cleaning, cooking), commercial (income generating) and community (politics, preparing for weddings))?

? Are these carried out equally by each socio-economic group?

? Which has more status?

Hints

For the 24 hour clock, check when the "day" starts - for some it is at midnight, for others sunrise/6 am, for others, sunset.

If all the people work for the same organization, ask some participants to imagine they are teachers, politicians, farmers, construction workers, mothers, hotel managers or flood defence managers.

Note: this person does not appear to cook or clean...

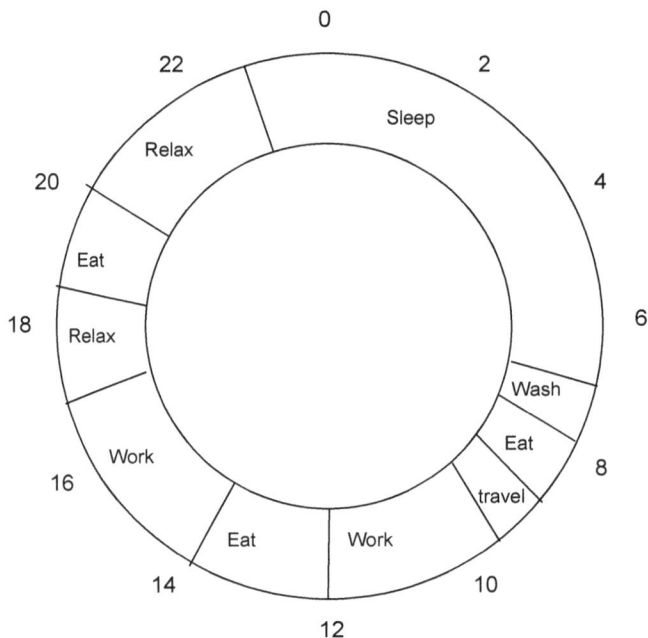

Figure 4. Example of a time chart

Note: this person has work and house work, with a month's holiday in August

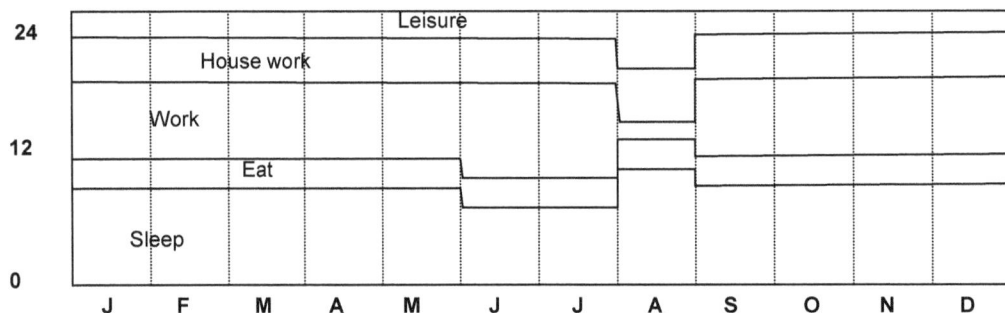

Figure 5. Example of a calendar

Unit 8:
How is the work shared out?

Purpose

To show that men and women may have different work responsibilities

Gender message

Women often have the less prestigious jobs, domestic tasks and often a motive for ensuring safe water supplies and sanitation.

Engineering message

Engineers need to know who uses infrastructure so they design it to suit.

Materials

Worksheets and pens

Time

30 minutes

Either as a large group, or in small groups, ask the participants to fill in the table of responsibilities.

■ For *who*? they can put:

  – Men ♂, women ♀ or both ♀ ♂, or

  – some idea of the social status of people (high, medium or low), or

  – paid or unpaid, or

  – skilled or unskilled.

■ For *where*? they can put:

  – at home, at work, elsewhere

■ For *when*? they can put:

  – in the "working day", outside work hours

In a general discussion, ask:

? Summarize the outputs, are there any trends?

? Are all the tasks relevant?

? Have any tasks been missed off?

? What information does this provide other participants (e.g. different people in society carry out different jobs).

? What information does this provide project managers (e.g. differences between social groups, who to discuss particular tasks with)

? What information does this provide engineers? (e.g. who will be using infrastructure, who to discuss designs with)

? Does it raise the awareness of socio-economic issues?

If this was being carried out by a low income community:

? What types of work would be recorded? (domestic (cleaning, cooking), commercial (income generating) and community (politics, preparing for weddings))?

? Are these carried out equally by each socio-economic group?

? Which has more status?

Hints

You can add extra tasks to the list - both relevant to the context and totally irrelevant.

If you split into small groups, ask one to analyse the tasks by gender, another by social status etc. and then compare lists.

Table 2: Examples of a responsibility matrix			
What	Who	When	Where
Washing clothes			
Paying water bills			
Having a shower			
Washing the car			
Washing the windows			
Bathing the children			
Changing soiled babies			
Managing a water utility			
Designing a water supply			
Building a water supply			
Preparing vegetables			
Watering the garden			
Watering livestock			
Cleaning the toilet			
Going to the toilet			
Unblocking sewers			
Recycling rubbish			
Putting rubbish out to be collected			
Paying for rubbish collection			
Collecting rubbish			
Disposing of rubbish			
?			
?			
?			

Unit 9:
Census

Purpose

To show that a census obtains factual information but there may be flaws.

Gender message

Census information needs to be disaggregated (collected separately for men and women).

Census data may provide factual information, but cannot measure perceptions.

Collecting census data does not enhance the status of women by itself.

Engineering message

Censuses provide factual information, but may miss out details and people's perceptions.

Materials

Pen and paper.

Time

30 minutes

Ask a small group to provide details of their group, for the following parameters:

- Height
- Weight
- Age
- Educational level
- Shoe size
- Sex
- Family size
- Other relevant information etc.

In a discussion, ask:

? What are the averages for each parameter?

? Is this representative of the small group?

? Is this representative of all the participants?

? Is this representative of the wider community?

? Is all the information useful for engineering design?

? Are all the questions clear? (e.g. what is meant by family - do you mean a household?)

? Do you know the answers to all the questions (e.g. how accurate are the heights?)

? Did you give the correct answers to all the questions (e.g. people may be reluctant to provide their weights or age)?

? What information is not provided? (e.g. opinions, feelings, priorities)

? Does the exercise change attitudes or give information to the participants?

Hints

> *Does one size fit all? Do we design for the average sized person, the top (or bottom) 95%. What parameter do we use? In designing a door we need to know the height of the person, the width and where their hand is (to position the handle) - are height, weight and hand position directly related?*

Chose people who are obviously not representative of the group, or who have widely differing heights for example.

Unit 10:
Whose perspective?

Purpose

To show that the same concept/fact can be looked at in a variety of ways.

Gender message

Men and women may look at the same problem in a different way, due to different (cultural/educational/social) perspectives.

Engineering message

Engineers have one perspective on a subject. Others may have different priorities.

Materials

A large piece of paper or just mark on the floor in chalk, sticks or scratch into the soil.

Time

20 minutes

On a large sheet of paper, draw a letter "W". Position two people on each of the four sides of the paper and ask them to describe what they see.

? Is it a "W", an "M", a "3", an "E"?

? Perhaps it is the Greek letter "Σ" (sigma) or the Chinese character 山 (mountain)?

? Is it a picture of something?

> *The perspective does not only depend on the physical viewpoint, but the education and background of the viewer. We should not assume that our viewpoint, priorities or assumptions are shared by everybody.*

Hints

If the group is mixed (e.g. men/women, literate/non-literate, different nationalities), use this to see if there are different interpretations.

Do people turn their heads to see the "W" the "right" way up?

The exercise may not provide technical information, but can show that people cannot assume they have the full picture

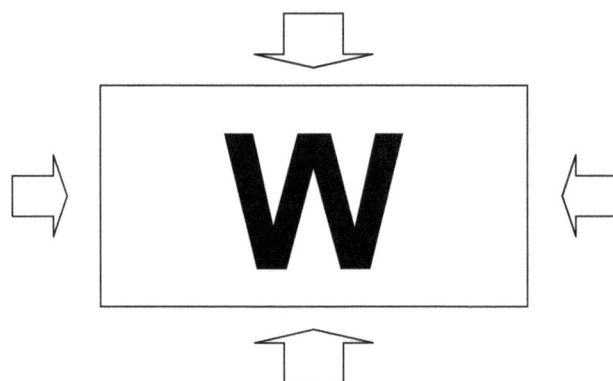

Figure 6. Testing viewpoints

Unit 11:
Who knows what?

Purpose

*To raise awareness
that assumptions about
knowledge can be
misleading.*

Gender message

*Men and women can be
aware of different issues.
Communication should not
assume that both parties are
totally aware of each other's
priorities.*

*This shows both men and
women that they have
knowledge and priorities that
the other group may not be
aware of.*

Engineering
message

*Engineers need to find out
information from others, but
also need to tell people what
they are doing.*

Materials

*Diagrams and explanations
drawn onto A4 paper, or use
role play.*

Time

30 minutes

Give a small group of people a copy of Johari's windows (named after researchers **Jo**seph Luft and **Ha**rry Ingham).

Allow them to look at the pictures and decide what they represent. Many participative tools rely on visual techniques to get a message across. Johari's window was developed to show how two people/groups could have different awareness and knowledge of issues. This has been adapted to show how people inside/outside a community (men/women, rich/poor) have different understandings of an issue.

Another visual technique often used is role play (acting a story or situation). Ask the group to act out a scene that demonstrates each of the four situations to the rest of the group. Either have one group per situation or one group can demonstrate all four scenarios.

Examples include:

- Unknown: Future consumption of water - the two parties need to talk to together to see how improved access to water may or may not change consumption

- Hidden: Women will continue to use an open pool for drinking water because they do not like the taste of the groundwater.

- Blind: The engineer can see that basic sanitation will improve living conditions in a slum, but the local people do not realise what a beneficial impact latrines will have.

- Open: Irrigation will increase crop yields during the dry season.

In a discussion, discuss:

? Do you understand that there are issues that you are not aware of? - give some examples

? Are there issues that you know about and assume incorrectly that everybody understands and accepts them?

? Of the four scenarios, which is the optimum position to be in?

? How can you get there (communication - listening and talking - including listening for things that are not there)

? How effective is role play; do you feel comfortable doing it?

? How effective is the use of the pictures; do they need additional explanation?

Hints

Role-play needs people who are willing to take part, select people who you think are willing to have a go.

Example of Johari window

Redraw the picture using appropriate people. One person (shown here with glasses) is "external", "powerful" or "expert". The other is "local". The local could be poor, female, of a different class/caste/religion/race.

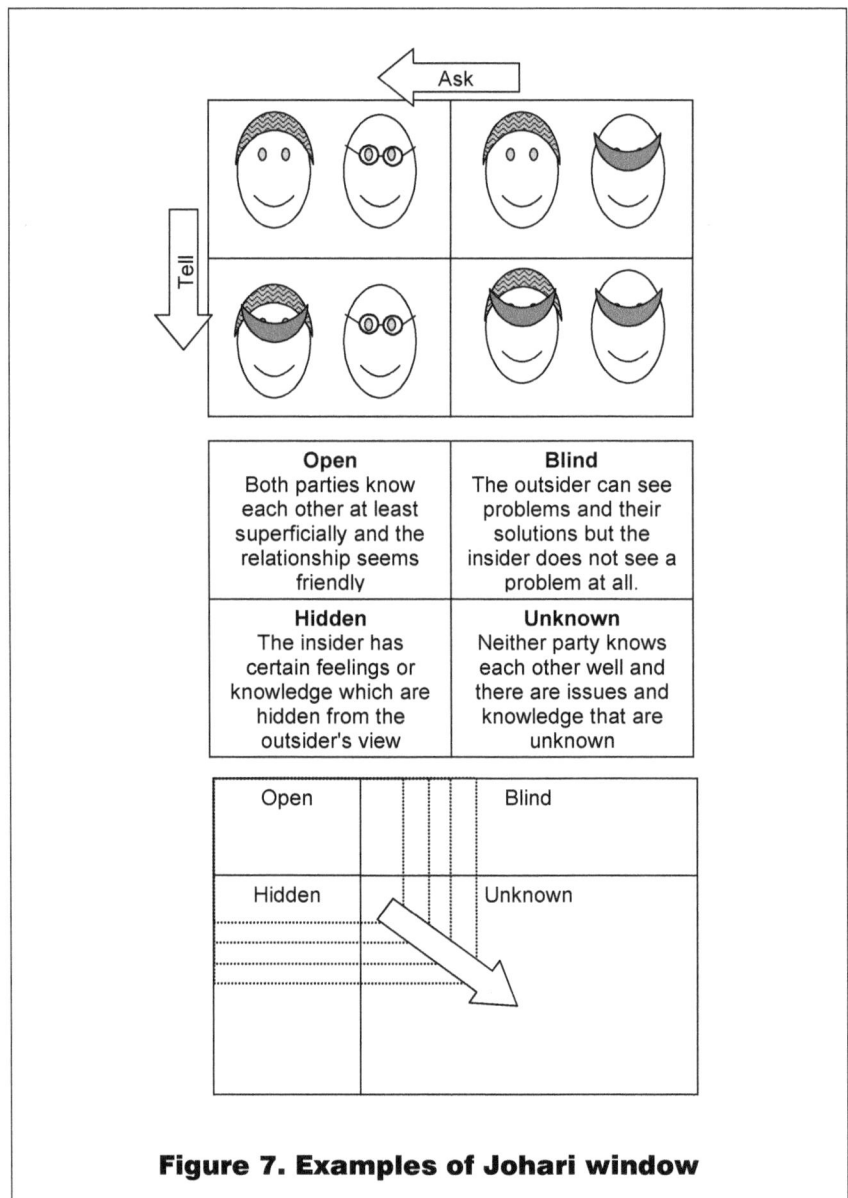

Figure 7. Examples of Johari window

Unit 12:
Designing a tap stand

Purpose

To show that people can be excluded from decision-making process.

Even a simple piece of infrastructure has many stakeholders.

Gender message

Women often get excluded from decision-making but may be key stakeholders.

Engineering message

Engineering issues may not be decided solely for engineering reasons.

Materials

Large paper or board.

Time

30-60 minutes (it takes 10 minutes to start but can be allowed to run on)

Draw a tap stand on the wall (or stand around an existing one). Assign each member of the group one or more of the roles listed below: You can add roles or change them to suit local circumstances. Some people have identified roles and need to identify themselves. Some people need to be assigned houses (e.g. a, b and c on the map); they do not need to identify themselves. Others have instructions not to speak. Do not tell everybody that some people are constrained from speaking - see if they notice. Tell the project manager that he/she has to run a community meeting to establish the dimensions of the tap stand and the location of the tap stand in an imaginary village. A sample village map is provided, but you can make your own, based on local conditions.

After at least 20 minutes (you can let it go on longer) stop the exercise. In a discussion, ask:

? did they come up with a size and location for the tap stand? - if so, is everybody happy?

? did the group notice that some people did not take part in the discussion?

? how did the people excluded from the discussion feel?

? If the decision was the engineer's only, where would the tap be? - is this the best place?

? how could the process be improved e.g.

■ separate meetings for socially excluded people,

■ cost benefit analysis of economic impact (supply crops or animals or both?),

■ broaden the technical options (more than one tap-stand, rainwater harvesting, private taps for people if they pay for them),

■ empowerment exercises for everybody to raise awareness of socially excluded people.

Hints

This is role play; the participants need to be relaxed and out of formal management positions.

Give some of the "excluded" roles to people who normally take a lead in discussions.

This unit can take a long time, as many people will be trying to make their voice heard. It needs to last long enough for it to become obvious that some people are not taking part in the discussion.

Table 3: List of roles			
1. You want to wash clothes	2. You want to wash children *(you can only speak once, unless asked to speak again)*	3. You want to wash yourself	4. You want to use the water for growing crop
5. You want to use the water for animals	6. You are worried about water quality	7. You are the **tap attendant** and get billed for wasted water *(you can only speak once, unless asked to speak again)*	8. You use a bucket to collect water *(you can only speak once, unless asked to speak again)*
9. You use a jerry can to collect water *(you can only speak once, unless asked to speak again)*	10. You use a oil drum to collect water	11. You are **in charge of spare parts** and do not want to store lots of different fittings	12. You are a **caretaker** and want to keep the area clean
13. You are the **treasurer** and want to make sure it will last for a long time without repairs	14. You are the **builder** and know that concrete gets washed away after a while.	15. You want to chat to your friends at the tap stand, but you don't want to be seen hanging around	16. You want the tap stand somewhere that is safe *(you can only speak once, unless asked to speak again)*
17. Your children will be collecting the water *(you can only speak once, unless asked to speak again)*	18. You are the **designer** and want to know the dimensions of the tap stand	19. You are the **project manager** and want to keep the meeting as short as possible	20. You want to be able to connect a hose pipe to the tap and have a supply in your house (d)
21. You carry the water container on your head *(you can only speak once, unless asked to speak again)*	22. You carry the water container on your back *(you can only speak once, unless asked to speak again)*	23. You carry the water container on a donkey	24. You carry the water container on a bicycle
25. You are a **local politician** and want votes	26. You want the tap outside your restaurant (a)	27. You want the tap outside your house (b)	28. You want the tap outside your house (c)
29. You want to limit consumption as the resource is limited	30. You are the owner of a nearby well that you charge people for using	31. You are a poor woman and do not like speaking in a meeting, so don't say anything. If asked, say you don't know	32. You are a **social scientist** and want to make sure everybody has a say.

For less than 32 people, pair up some of the roles, so some people have two issues that they want to get across (e.g. 3+14, 6+28, 10+26, 11+20, 13+27, 18+29). For more than 32, give two people the same role, starting with the socially excluded roles (e.g. 2, 21,22, 31 etc), so they are in the majority. People with roles in **bold** should identify themselves.

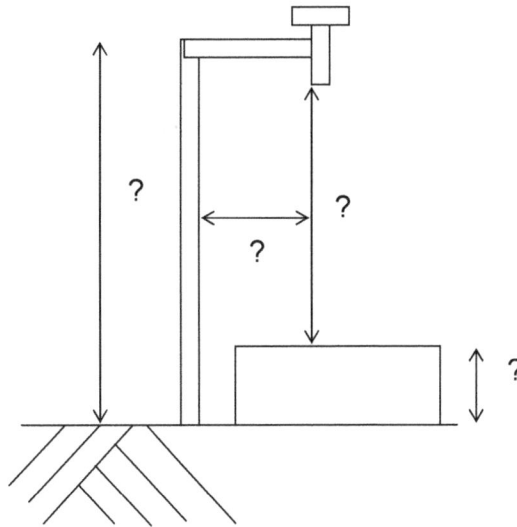

Figure 8. Diagram of tap stand

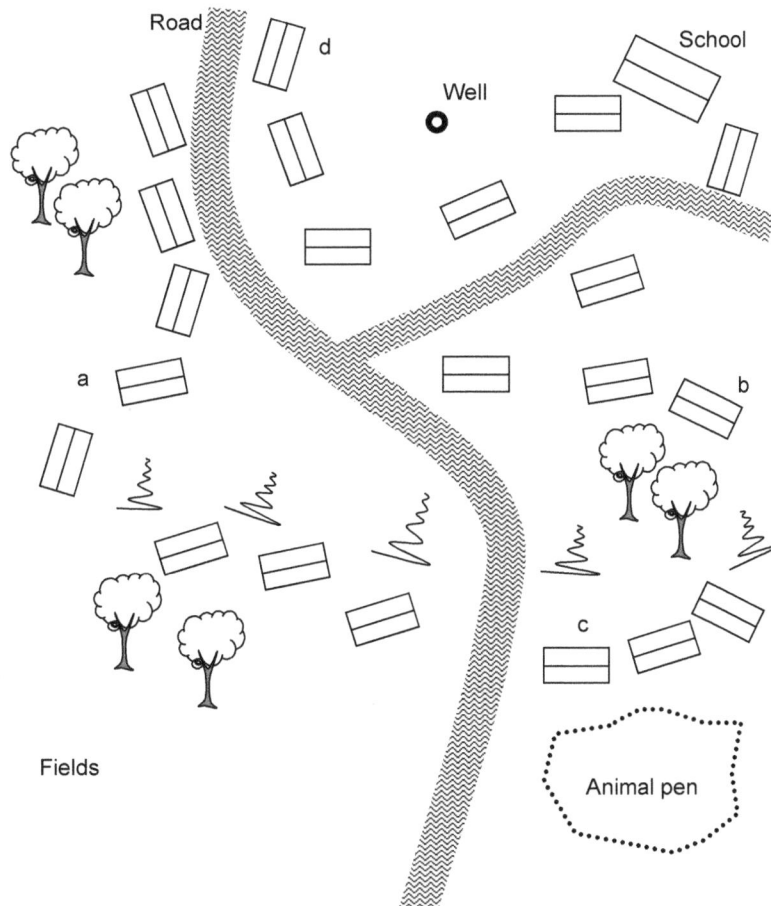

The rectangles are houses. Trees, a well, a school, two roads, fields, animal pens and a slope are also shown. The slope shown has the hill at the bottom of the diagram.

Road

d

Well

School

a

b

c

Fields

Animal pen

Figure 9. Diagram of village

Unit 13:
The engineering process

Purpose

To show that there are different methods of producing the same engineering product.

Gender message

The way in which a project is managed can have an impact on vulnerable groups.

Engineering message

Engineers control the project process as well as determining the final project.

Materials

None

Time

Preparation time 20 minutes or in participants' own time.

Allow 5-10 minutes per presentation.

> *Infrastructure developments normally concentrate on what is being built, rather than how it is planned, designed and constructed.*

Consider different construction procedures

1. Building a water supply/sewer/road using an international contractor

2. Building a water supply/sewer/road using small local contractors

3. Building a water supply/sewer/road using voluntary labour.

Divide the participants into three groups: Each group has to promote one option, pointing out the advantages and disadvantages of each option. They should give a presentation to "sell" their particular option. Consider;

? What does each cost?

? What is the impact on work quality?

? What changes would need to be made to the design?

? What changes would need to be made to the contract?

? Who does the work (especially the involvement of vulnerable people)?

? Where do the profits go?

? Who "owns" the work?

? Who takes technical decisions?

? What is the relationship with the funder/user?

Though voluntary labour may be seen as involving people directly, it can sometimes be seen as forced labour, with the less influential doing the work. It may also mean women have to do jobs that they would not normally do.

Each smaller group gives a presentation to the rest of the participants to sell their proposed procurement method. Allow time for general discussion afterwards. There is not necessarily a correct answer.

Hints

If the course runs over a couple of days, this could be given as an exercise to prepare in the evening.

If the is not much time, the presentations could be replaced by a general discussion about the pros and cons of each option.

Unit 14:
The project cycle

Purpose

To introduce the project cycle and how it appears from different perspectives.

Gender message

Vulnerable groups may not be included in some stages of the project cycle and so may not be able to influence decision-making.

Engineering message

Engineers are key players for part of the project cycle, but other people are involved before and after them.

Materials

Board or large sheet of paper

Time

20 minutes

There are a variety of models of how the engineering process works.

- Engineers will be familiar with progress charts. On a chart, list what activities take place, how long each takes, who is involved and the costs of each stage of a conventional project. This is a linear process.

- Planners and policy makers often view the project as a cycle, with policy and planning stages before the feasibility stage and evaluation and extensions after the project has been built and commissioned.

- On another chart, draw the project cycle with these extra stages, who is involved, how long it takes and what each stage costs. This is a circular process.

- Now consider the point of view of a user. At one extreme, they will not be involved until the project is finished. This is a point, rather than a linear or circular process.

Discuss the three models of the project process.

? At what stage are the major decisions made? (planning)

? When are engineers in charge of the project? (design, construction and perhaps operation)

? How can users shape their own projects? - should they be involved in policy, design or construction? (be involved earlier in planning and design, be involved later in operation and maintenance)

Strategic action is needed so vulnerable groups can influence policy. This will take a long time as the social barriers to their involvement in policy formulation have to be reduced. However, engineers can promote the status in the shorter term of these people by:

- Listening to them, showing that their opinion is valued

- Including their needs in the design, recognising their opinions

- Providing them with increased choice in how they manage their own lives.

- Providing equal opportunities for work and training - especially within the engineering organization

- Including discussion of social exclusion stakeholder analysis in training

Practical actions make the lives of vulnerable groups less difficult. The actions that engineers can provide are the same as the ones listed above.

Hints

Different visual methods could be used to illustrate the process, with different arrow lengths for time, different thickness for cost.

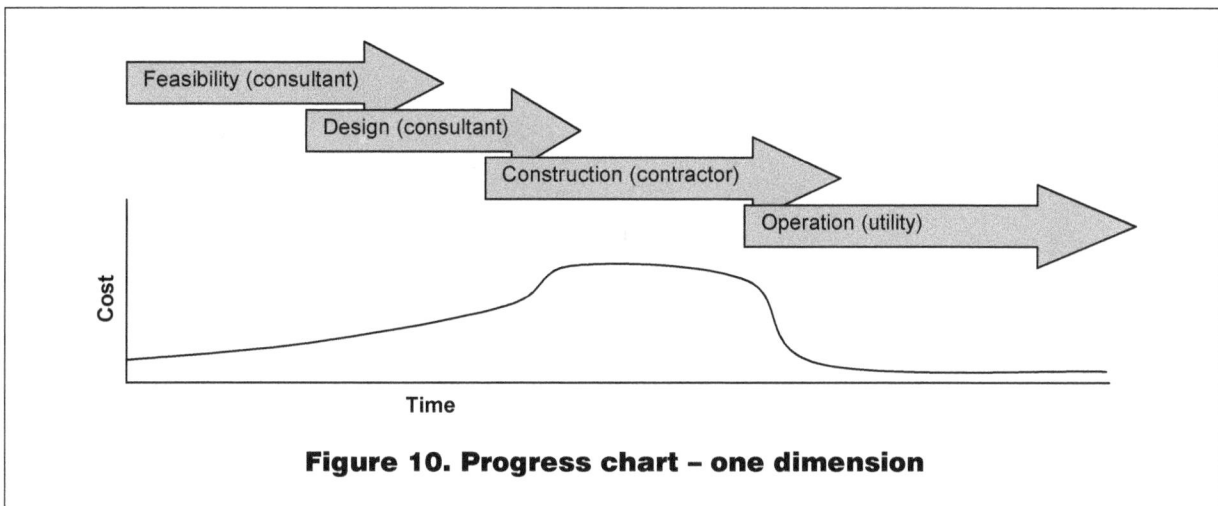

Figure 10. Progress chart – one dimension

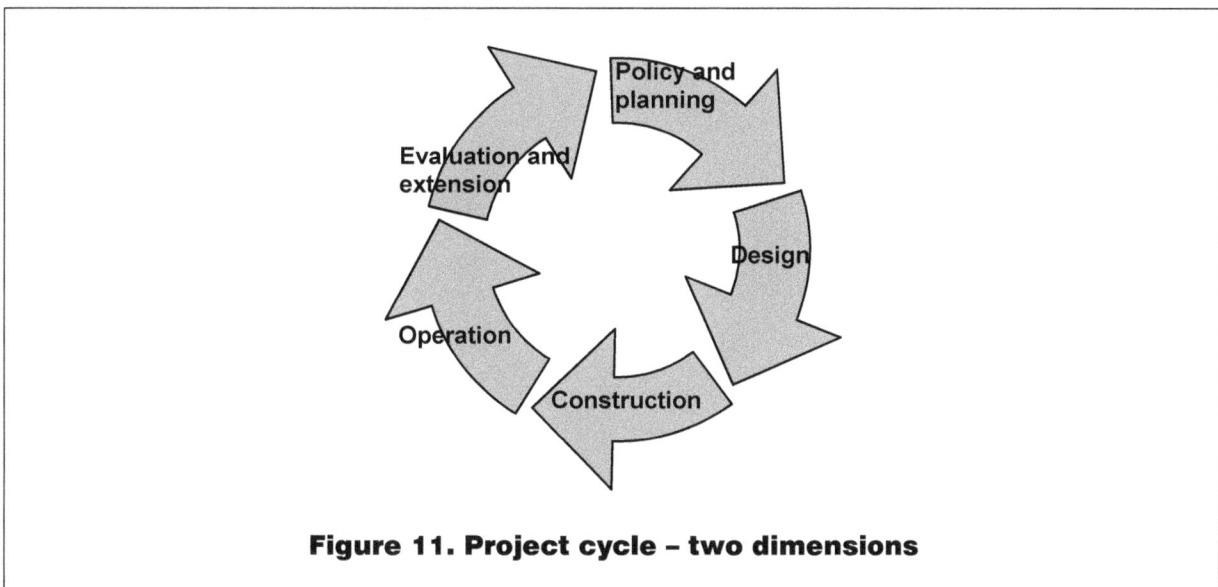

Figure 11. Project cycle – two dimensions

Development
by others

Use

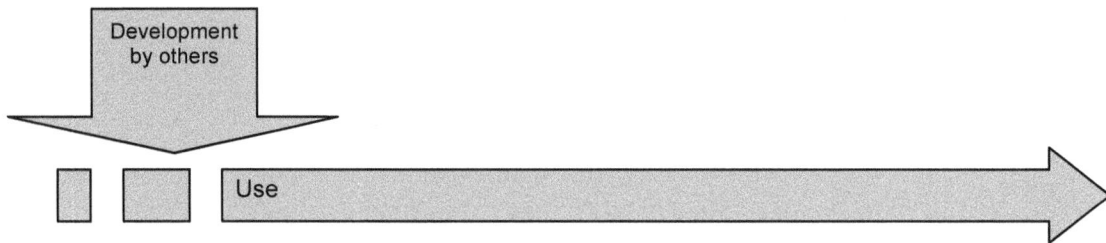

Figure 12. Users' viewpoint – single point?

Unit 15:
Engineering information

Purpose

To consider the ways we gather information and how effective this is.

Gender message

How we gather information can exclude groups of people.

Engineering message

How we gather information can exclude groups of people.

Materials

Paper and pens, board

Time

30 minutes

Census information may prove facts, but not perceptions or wishes of the users. Participative tools may indicate perceptions but may not necessarily provide technical data or inform the population about infrastructure options. Participative techniques may also prove problematic when dealing with large urban communities in cash-based economies rather than smaller groups in rural situations.

Divide in to two (or and even number) groups. Ask one group to consider censuses, topographic/geological surveys and other conventional engineering information gathering techniques, and the other to consider participative exercises. Pose the following questions:

? Who owns the process?

? Is the flow of information one way or two way?

? Who learns from the process?

? Who sets the questions?

? What about issues that are outside the survey?

? Who is being asked (household head - is that representative)?

? Can you ask the whole of the community?

? Is anybody left out?

? How long does this take?

? Does it promote consensus?

? How long does it take?

? Is it "rural" or "urban"?

? How accurate is it?

Ask the two groups to compare the results of their discussions (e.g.

prepare a table of positive and negative aspects of each group of methods).

Both methods have positive and negative aspects. Ideally, information techniques should maximise the positive aspects. In reality, there is not a divide between the techniques, but they form a continuos range from very "scientific" to very emotional.

Hints

This also could be set as "home work" to presented at a later date, with each participant completing a table e.g.

	Benefits	Problems
Engineering techniques		
Participative techniques		

Unit 16:
Customer surveys

Purpose

To introduce the ideas of customer surveys and how they can influence the engineering product.

Gender message

Women are an important proportion of the customers for infrastructure.

Engineering message

Engineers produce a product that should meet customers' needs.

Materials

None

Time

20 minutes

> *This unit is a short introduction to marketing and meeting the customers' needs.*

In marketing any product, various factors have to be considered. These are sometimes called the "7 P's" of marketing[4]. Infrastructure is a product just like soft drinks (sodas/minerals), with customers. Building infrastructure is inefficient if is does not meet the customers' needs. Consider:

- Product (the technical, service, maintenance and payment options)

- Price (tariff structure, profits, incentives, willingness to pay)

- Promotion (advertising, customer relations, meetings, demonstrations)

- Place (different products for different locations)

- People (two way communication, understanding, feedback, liaison with groups)

- Process (quality control, agreeing 7Ps, service reliability, streamlined service)

- Presence (accessibility by customers, image of project offices/ officers)

? Ask for relevant, local examples of each of these issues.

These will be influenced by people's previous experience (or lack of experience) and the perceptions and understanding will differ from community to community and between different social groups within the community.

Various methods can be used to find out the customers' needs. Consulting the whole population is both expensive and unnecessary. A representative sample may provide sufficient information and dialogue. Different groups (based on age, gender, wealth, education etc.) will need to be identified to ensure that the whole population is represented. Some groups may exist as established groups (e.g.

---

[4]   From Brassington and Pettitt (2000).

women's groups, school classes, and councillors) but others may have to created (e.g. meetings at clinics, water sources). Because not all the population is involved, wider promotion of the issues discussed may have to be carried out (posters, radio etc.).

The methods used can vary from a list of questions to participative exercises used elsewhere in the training material. Compromise methods include:

- structured interviews; a set of predetermined questions are used to promote discussion but also give information and perceptions about specific issues.

- focus groups; a group of people is asked to discuss a particular issue. This can provide a greater insight into general issues and ideas the project team are not aware of, but may not give such concrete answers as a more structured approach.

It is important that the sessions are prepared thoroughly, with the whole project team selecting relevant questions. Questions can either be direct (*"where do you currently get water from?"*), indicative (*"what is your house built of?" - indicates income and priority of improving their home*), relative (*"which of these five options would you prefer"* or *"please rank these four options in order of preference"*).

The sessions should be piloted, to check that the questions yield information that is useful and relevant. The work should be carried out by trained personnel, to ensure that the sessions work smoothly, but also that technical, social and economic information can be explored.

The process can be iterative, with the design being refined in stages.

Hints

This introduction to adopting a customer/market based approach, could be used as an exercise, with participants being asked to draw up:

A: Aspects of marketing infrastructure (especially a specific project), based on the 7Ps

B: Methods of putting the Process/People/Promotion aspects into practice, using participative, non-participative and other ways of gathering information.

Unit 17:
Problem and objective trees

Purpose

To identify project priorities at an early stage.

Gender message

Using focus groups from different sectors of the community can demonstrate the diversity of opinion.

Engineering message

The people should determine project objectives with a stake in the final outcome.

There may be a variety of project objectives.

Materials

Card and pens

Time

30 minutes for each tree.

Problem trees

For this unit you need to set the context, either role playing villagers' concerns (in which case you will need to assign roles - see xxxx) or based on the participants' direct experience (e.g. transport to work, job security, health care or education). With groups of between six to twelve participants, record the problems they face on card or other material. Symbols can be used if preferred. The results are then sorted, with similar problems being grouped together in piles. The causes and effects of each problem are then discussed. This can lead to additional cards being added and some being discarded. Finally, the problem cards are arranged to show their interrelationships. (see example[5]).

The facilitator should not lead the exercise by concentrating on a particular issue when those participating have other concerns, but some guidance will stop the problem tree becoming too large. For example, it is important to know whether people are more interested in economic opportunities than potable water if their demands are to be recognised. The unit shows the breadth of activities that need to be considered.

When the group agrees that it represents their collective perceptions, the cards are stuck down and lines drawn to show the links between them.

Objective trees

It is a relatively simple exercise to transform a problem statement into an objective, simply by rephrasing it. In the same way, a problem tree can be inverted into an objective tree (see example below). This links the problems people face with the decisions they will make. Involving people in decision-making is only likely to be effective if those decisions are felt to be relevant. The exercise highlights the constraints that all projects face and introduces a certain amount of reality into the process - it is unlikely that every objective can be addressed.

---

[5] The example for this exercise is taken from "Designing water supply and sanitation projects to meet demand" Deverill et al. WEDC, 2002.

In the full group, discuss:

? Does this exercise help define a project?

? When should it be carried out? (early in the project cycle)

? How can socially excluded groups be involved? (separate meetings at appropriate times)

? What is the engineer's response? (be prepared to alter plans, re-organise priorities, programmes and budgets)

Hints

This is a very open exercise, like brainstorming. The aim is to identify issues rather than solve them at this stage.

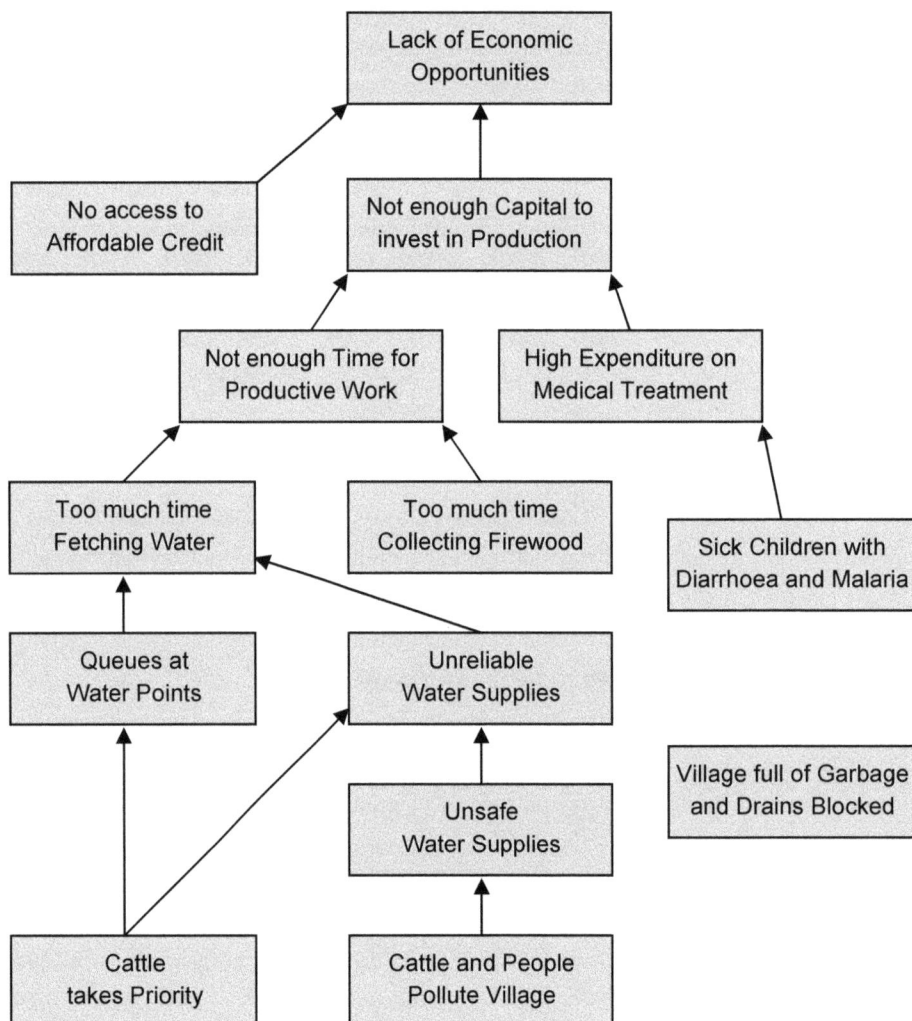

Figure 13. Example of a problem tree

The shaded objectives are those which have been incorporated into a water and sanitation project

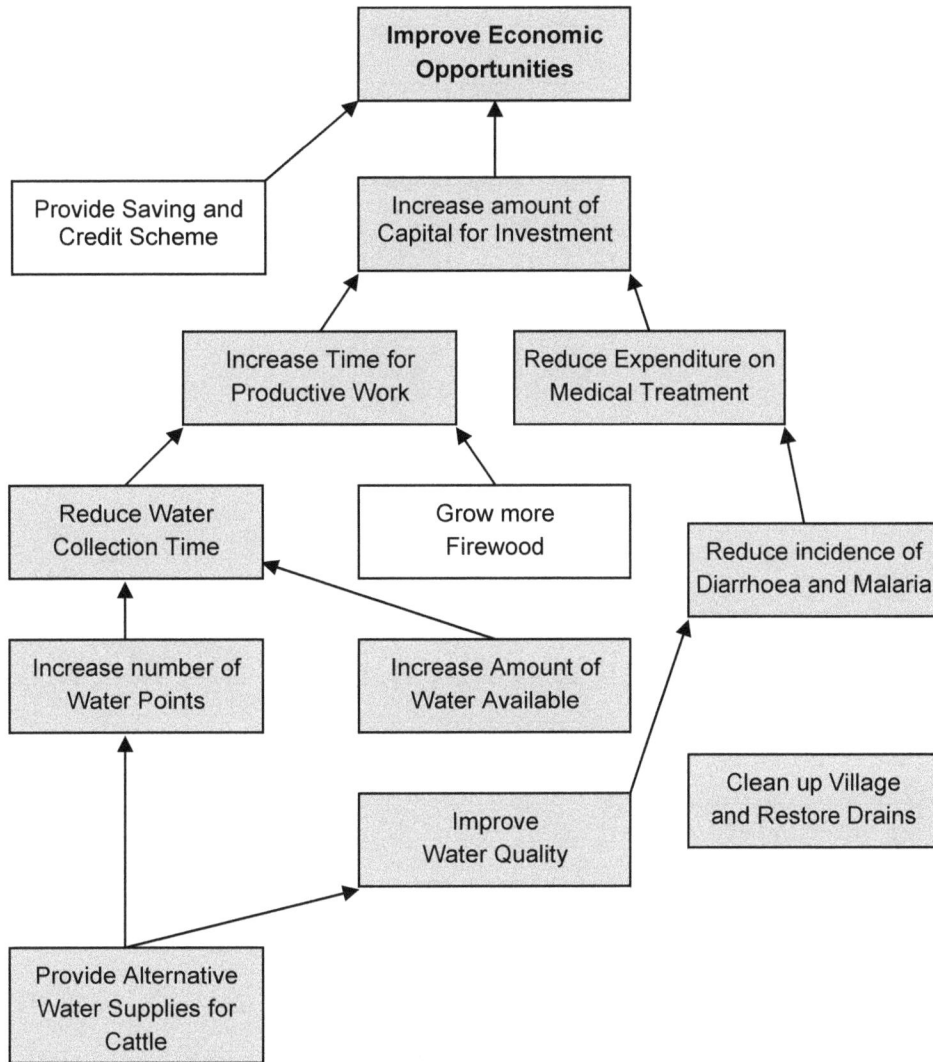

Figure 14. Example of an objective tree

Issue - journey to work: the problems

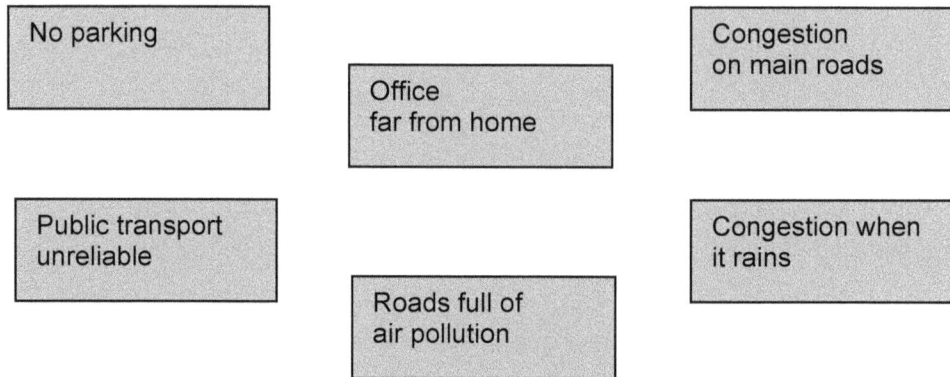

No parking		Congestion on main roads
	Office far from home	
Public transport unreliable		Congestion when it rains
	Roads full of air pollution	

Issue - journey to work: the objectives

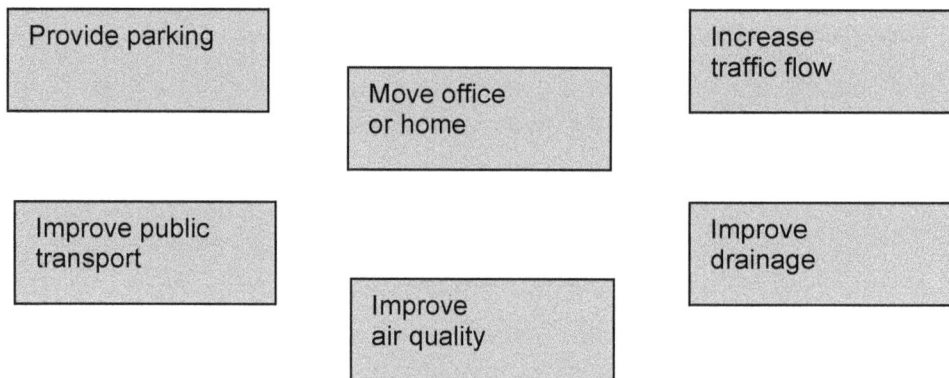

Provide parking		Increase traffic flow
	Move office or home	
Improve public transport		Improve drainage
	Improve air quality	

Figure 15. Alternative problem trees

Unit 18:
Faeces, fingers and food

Purpose

To look at technical and social methods of reducing the spread of disease via faecal/oral routes.

Gender message

Men and women prevent diseases spreading in different ways.

The main managers in controlling one disease route should have influence over all aspects.

Engineering message

Infrastructure services are physical structures and human activity

Services work best when the management is not split between organizations.

Materials

Paper, pens and somewhere to display the flow diagram (wall, notice board or floor)

Time

30 minutes

Problem trees

Write the words [faeces], [fluids (or water)], [fields], [flies], [fingers], [food] and [face (or mouth)] on pieces of card or paper. Ask the group to arrange the cards and link them with arrows to show how disease can spread from faeces to the mouth via various routes. One possible solution is shown below. Do not let the flow diagram get too complex.

For each of the links, write a technical method of stopping the transfer of disease (e.g. sanitation, water treatment) and place these on the link (see example).

?   Are these technical solutions sufficient by themselves?

?   How can technical barriers be by-passed? (not managing water treatment plants, not using toilets, not washing hands)

For each of the links, write an activity that can stop the transfer of disease (e.g. hand washing, composting, food storage) and place these on the link.

?   Are these behaviour changes sufficient by themselves?

?   Is it a good idea to separate the management of technical and social barriers (no - it is no good designing sanitation if the people cannot use it correctly).

For each of the technical and social barriers, who is usually the key person in managing the barrier (e.g. men (managing a water treatment plant, women (managing food preparation, mothers teach children to wash hands). Write this on a card or colour the card (e.g. blue/pink) and put it next to the technical or social barrier (see example).

?   How can the management be made stronger? Example include:

■   do not divide responsibility,

■   encourage people to see the whole process so men understand women's roles and vice versa,

■   break down the divisions so the rigid divide between men and women's roles is reduced

Hints

A similar exercise could be carried out with transport, agriculture or fuel (or all three), developing the technical and socio-economic factors that are involved in preparing a meal (see example).

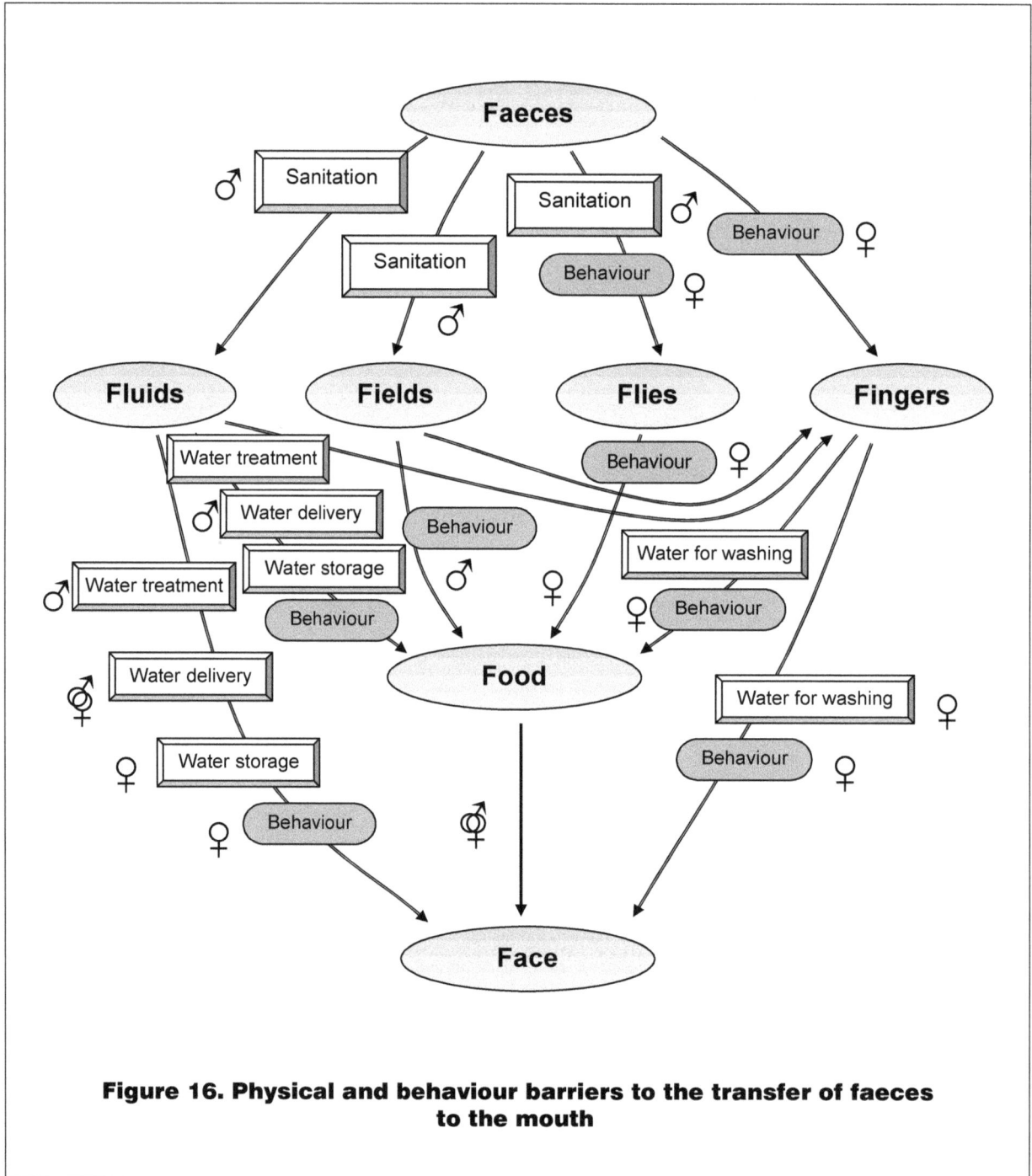

Figure 16. Physical and behaviour barriers to the transfer of faeces to the mouth

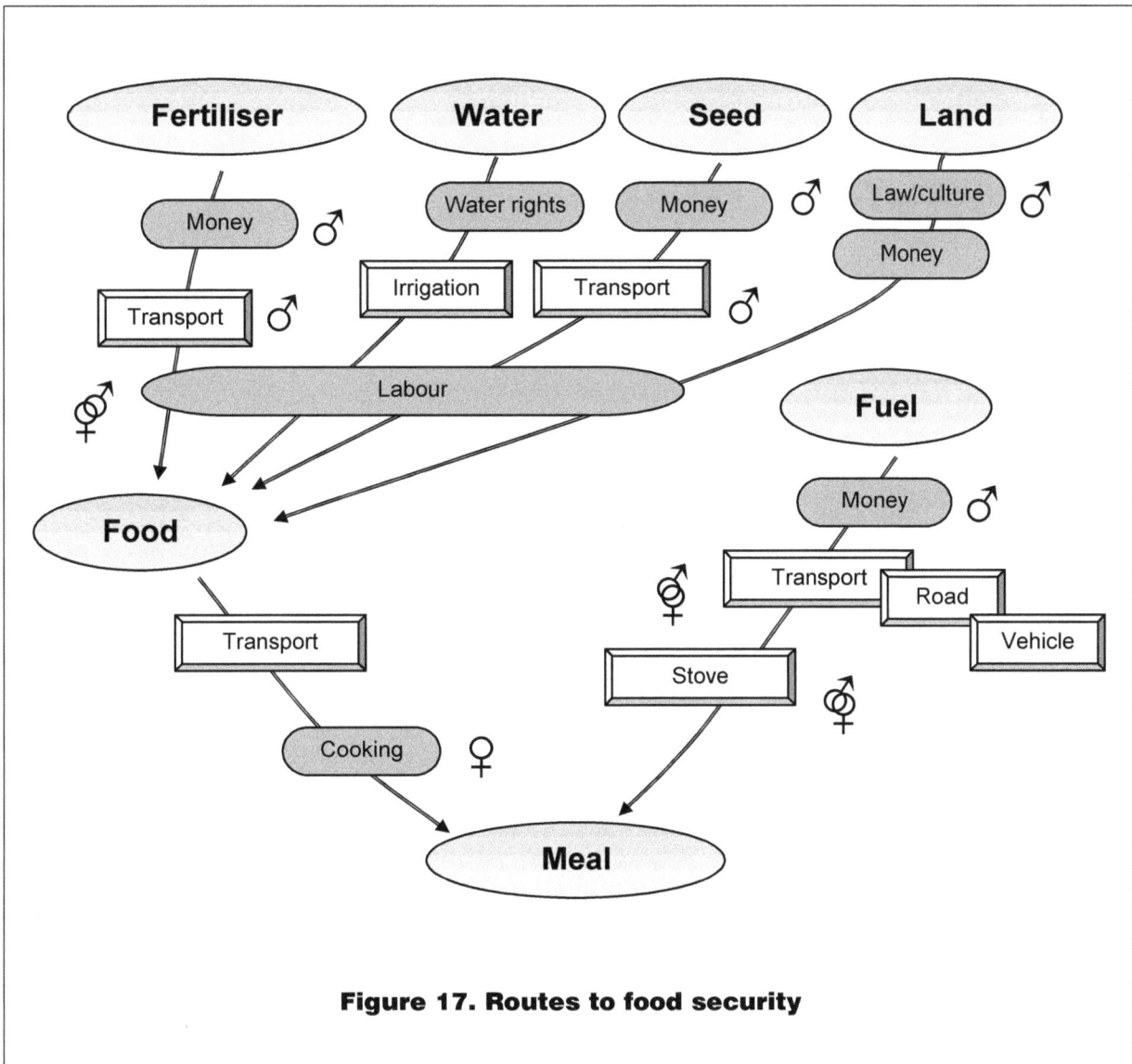

Figure 17. Routes to food security

Unit 19:
Community maps

Purpose

To show that social scientists and engineers gather similar information

Gender message

Infrastructure can be seen differently by men and women.

Engineering message

Infrastructure can be seen differently by men and women.

Materials

Copies of two community maps.

Time

20 minutes

Engineers are used to making maps and carrying out surveys. Social scientists often do the same thing. Ask the group to compare the two maps provided. If the group is large split the participants into smaller groups for this stage, to allow everybody to take part. Ask them to look for differences between the two maps and to list what engineering and social information is provided.

A community was asked to prepare village maps. Noticeable differences are[6]:

- the men have about 55 houses to the women's 73. This is because there were often two huts in each compound - one for the man and the other for his wife. However, both maps still missed out households that shared a compound.

- Each group categorised people by wealth and well being. Men had categories for wealth (ownership of houses, farms, livestock) and "god-fearing", an attribute worthy of respect. Women found that the "rich" and "poor" did not give accurate results, so they also categorised people by harvests.

With the full group, discuss:

? What are the differences/similarities between the two group's perceptions of their community - in terms of wealth and well being?

? What are the differences/similarities between the two group's perceptions of their community - in terms of infrastructure? (note men placed more emphasis on roads, buses, and paths but did not mark the garbage dump).

? What other information is needed to design various projects e.g.

- Drainage; where does it flood, flow routes, natural wetlands, erosion, siltation, muddy areas

- Sanitation; places where people want public latrines, places where latrines should not be placed (e.g. near holy areas), areas were faeces are dumped.

---

[6]   For a more detailed discussion, see *"Gendered Perceptions of Well-being in Darko, Ghana"* M Kaul Shah, in *"The Myth of Community"* Ed Gujit and Shah, IT Publications 1998.

- Solid waste: places where waste is dumped, blocked drains, places where rubbish is/is not collected; people who sort waste.

- Water; location of existing water points and water sources; households who need help with getting water (e.g. the old, the sick, widows, schools).

Hints

If a social scientist can provide locally produced community maps, this may be more relevant to the group.

For work with the community, where they prepare their own maps, select representative people (men/women, rich/poor) and a convenient time and place for that group. They can use any method of making a map (using stones or people to represent the situation) which can then be copied onto paper.

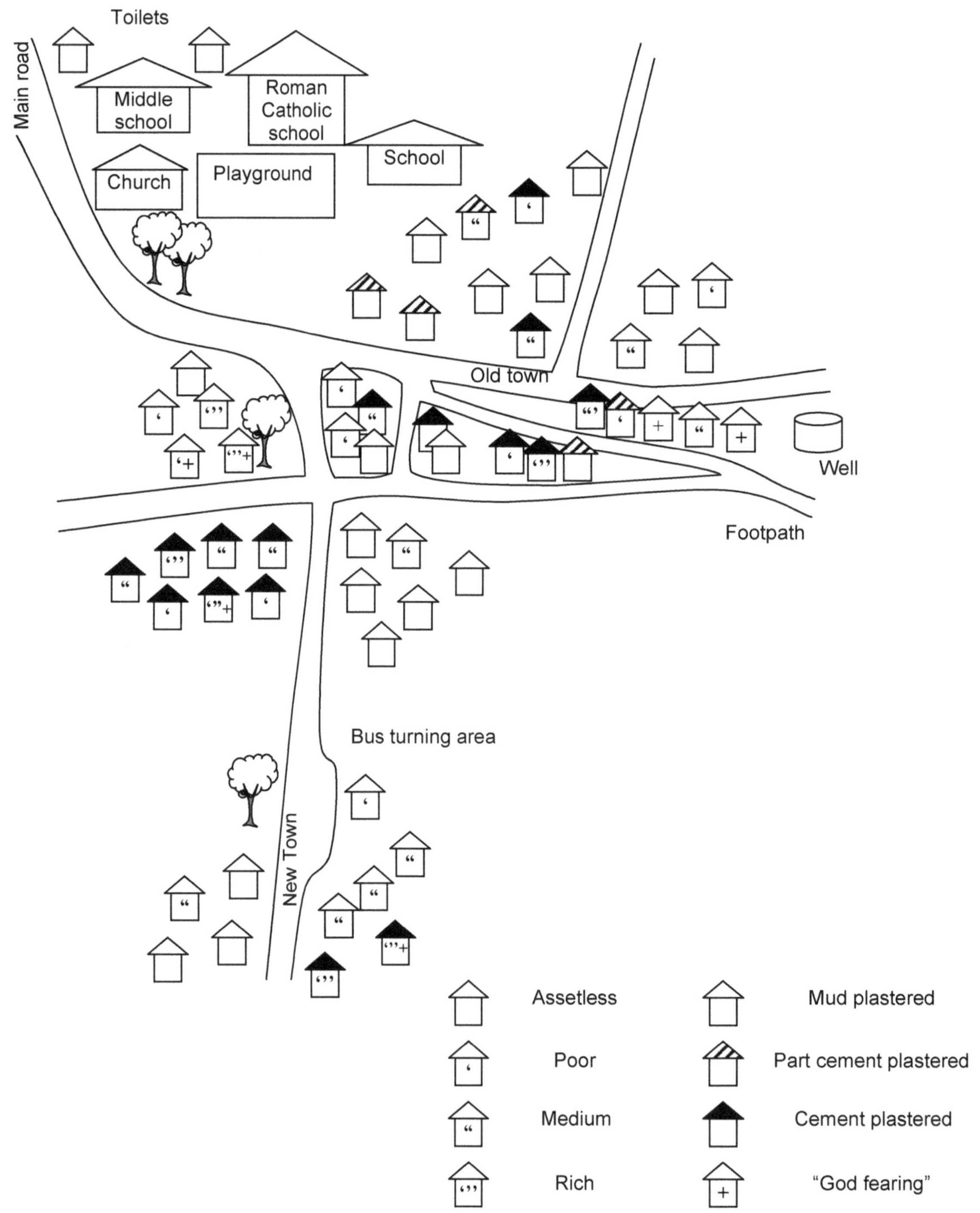
Toilets
Main road
Middle school
Roman Catholic school
Church
Playground
School
Old town
Well
Footpath
Bus turning area
New Town
Assetless
Mud plastered
Poor
Part cement plastered
Medium
Cement plastered
Rich
"God fearing"

Figure 18. Social map prepared by men[7]

[7] From *"Gendered Perceptions of Well-being in Darko, Ghana"* M Kaul Shah, in *"The Myth of Community"* Ed Gujit and Shah, IT Publications 1998.

Toilet   School

School

School

Playground

Road

Community farm

Traditional religion site

Garbage dump

Well

	High harvest		Rich		Cement plastered
H		L'			
M	Medium harvest	L"	Very rich		Half-cement plastered
L	Low harvest		Not plastered		Mud plastered

Figure 19. Social map prepared by women[8]

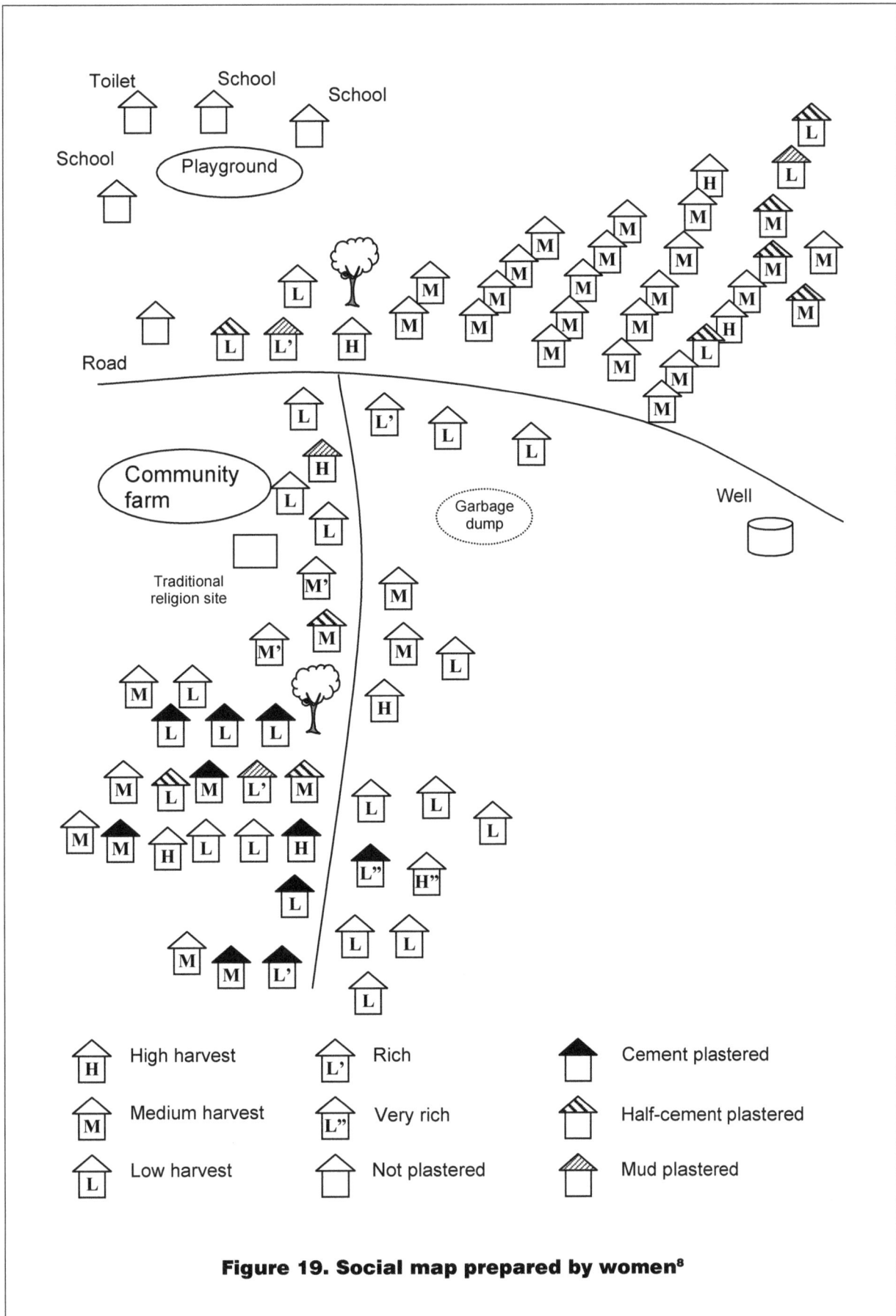

8   From *"Gendered Perceptions of Well-being in Darko, Ghana"* M Kaul Shah, in *"The Myth of Community"* Ed Gujit and Shah, IT Publications 1998.

Unit 20:
Site visit

Purpose

To show how a standard engineering procedure can be used to also look at social issues.

Gender message

Many differences between social groups can be identified by direct observation.

Engineering message

A site visit can be enhanced by talking to the local population.

Materials

None

Time

20 minutes

> *Engineers are used to conducting site visits and walking pipe routes or road alignments.*

Discuss what information is being looked for on a site visit. Examples include:

? Topography

? Physical obstacles, e.g. buildings

? Rivers, streams, drainage paths

? Rock types

? Access routes

? Available materials

> *Social scientists carry out a similar activity, called a **transect walk**. This looks at what people are doing and asks them what they think of existing facilities.*

What is the main difference in the way information is gathered by a social scientist? It is likely that they will talk to the residents and ask opinions and preferences rather than pure facts. Often they walk through the community in a straight line to get a more representative view of the community than a walk along the main streets.

Using a mixture of observation and discussion, a variety of information can be gathered:

▪ Where different people live - are the rich (or poor) all in one area?

▪ Proof of who is using water sources

▪ Asking about the reliability of the water sources, or presence of other sources

- Physical state of water points, latrines, solid waste management and if it is considered a problem.

- Asking what improvements would be welcomed

- Preferred routes for travel

This brings consultation to people, without them having to attend meetings, but some people, such as women, may be less willing to talk to strangers.

Hints

This unit shows how a standard engineering exercise, the site visit, has a "social" counterpart. The group may also identify other engineering exercises that can provide socio-economic information.

Site maps and cost/benefit analyses are other technical and social tools, although they are often applied separately by each discipline.

Unit 21:
Designing a pit latrine slab

Purpose

To demonstrate a method of engaging people in discussion about technical issues.

Gender message

Men and women use infrastructure in different ways, due to their sex and their socially determined roles.

Engineering message

People can help design their own infrastructure if they are asked correctly.

Materials

Sheet of paper and pen, or mark directly onto the floor or use a pit latrine platform without footrests.

Time

10 -20 minutes

Place a large sheet of paper on the floor, preferably on a smooth hard surface. Draw a keyhole in the centre of the paper. Ask each participant in turn to squat over the hole and draw around his or her feet. One person should pretend to be pregnant (e.g. have a heavy cushion tied to their stomach). Another person should pretend to have a problem with their leg and be unable to bend it much.

> *If the participants are all from one group, you need to explain that people of other ages/genders/ethnicities (even locally within regions)/ physical abilities may squat in a different position and need the footrests in another place.*

Discuss the results of the exercise.

? Does one size fit all?

? How about people who are not in the group - children, old people, men or women?

? Did other factors get raised (e.g. size of superstructure, need for grab rails, paint the footrests white for partially sighted people)

This can be used as a starting point for other discussions about designing latrines, e.g.

? does everybody use the same latrine or do men/ women/ children/ relatives use different latrines,

? are there other issues that should be considered - privacy/easy to clean/convenient/safe/snakes/hand washing/anal cleansing

? what else are latrines used for - washing/changing sanitary towels/ sex/smoking?

? what shouldn't they be used for - but are: hiding during school hours/bullying/storage/chicken sheds

Hints

This is a sensitive subject. Participants may prefer do this unit in single sex groups or even one at a time in private, with the results discussed in the whole group.

Draw just the slab (at least 600mmx600mm) and a keyhole.
The participants draw around each other's feet.

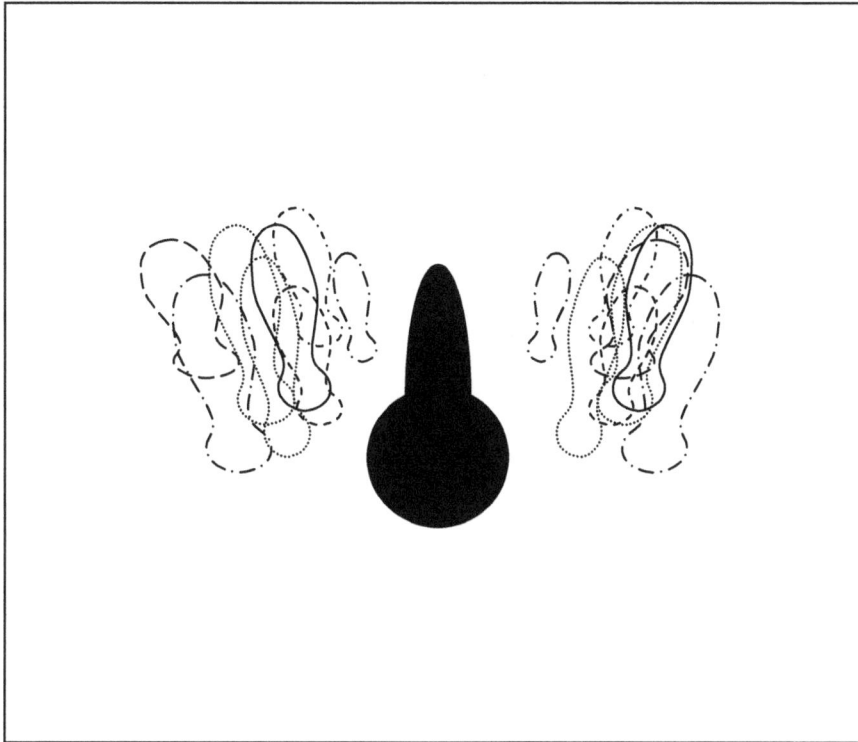

Figure 20. Drawing of a pit latrine slab

Unit 22:
Well wall design

Purpose

To show how participative methods can be used to develop technical specifications.

Gender message

Men and women can be involved in the development of their own infrastructure.

Men and women may have different design and operational criteria.

Engineering message

People can help design their own infrastructure if they are asked correctly.

Materials

A bucket, water and a pole/rope.

Time

20 minutes

This unit has four roles.
1. *To establish what the height of the well wall should be,*
2. *To establish who should be making that decision*
3. *To make it easier to talk about other design issues related to the well*
4. *To discuss operational/hygiene issues.*

Fill a bucket with water (it may be best to do this unit outside). Two people hold a rod or piece of string at about 2m high. This represents the wall of a well. Each participant tries to lift the bucket over the "wall" (see plan view). The rod should be lowered to 1.5, then 1 then 0.5 and finally 0.25 metres, with everybody having a go to lift the bucket over the "wall".

In a discussion, ask how high the wall should be. Should any particular group be given preference in selecting the height of the wall? (e.g. the people who will be using the well?). What are the other design considerations in setting the wall height (e.g. children/animals falling in, surface water pollution).

Have a general discussion about the design of the well.

? Do people use the well wall for placing their water container on before they put in on their head/back/bicycle? Are there any problems with this? (e.g., water spilling back into the well).

? Is the bucket used for drawing water put on the ground? (this will transfer dirt back into the well).

? How about other activities that may take place near the well (washing people/clothes/pots/chatting).

? How about access to the well - is it easy to get to in the wet season? Would steps/paths/handrails help?

Hints

The group could be divided in two (e.g. men and women) and the results of the two groups compared.

Choose somewhere where water can be split without causing damage and have something to wipe up split water.

Unit 23:
Getting the design across

Purpose

To show engineers a variety of methods of describing their designs.

> *Engineering drawing has been developed to provide clear information in a standard format, but it does require some training to read the drawing.*

Gender message

Communication techniques have to suit the audience, not the person preparing them.

Engineering message

People can help design their own infrastructure if they are asked correctly.

Materials

Drawing paper and pens

Time

20 minutes

- Draw a plan and two elevations of a simple latrine (based on local practice - e.g. round or square)

- Ask the participants to draw a three dimensional view of the superstructure (perspective not isometric).

- Add colour to show solid objects and shading to emphasise the perspective.

- Add a figure to show scale and some buildings or trees to show the context.

Discuss:

? What information is needed by:

   ? an engineer

   ? a builder

   ? a user (men, women, children)

? who is the best person to draw diagrams of the design (artists may have better drawing skills, engineers know the technical information they need to get across, social scientists may know of cultural practises that make the drawing relevant (e.g. dress, social indicators))?

? What other techniques could be used (ask for suggestions). E.g.

   ■ models made by the project team

   ■ models made by the different sections of the community

   ■ role plays (e.g. a play where different members of the household describe aspects of the latrine/water supply/road/stove)

- demonstration structures, where a variety of options are built for people to examine in more detail.

- site visits, taking representatives of the community to look at a variety of existing projects and allowing them to talk to the men, women and children who use them.

- Photographs of existing structures (although these are not as easy to understand as good drawings. Drawings allow details to be emphasised).

Hints

Try to get some good and bad examples of diagrams used locally.

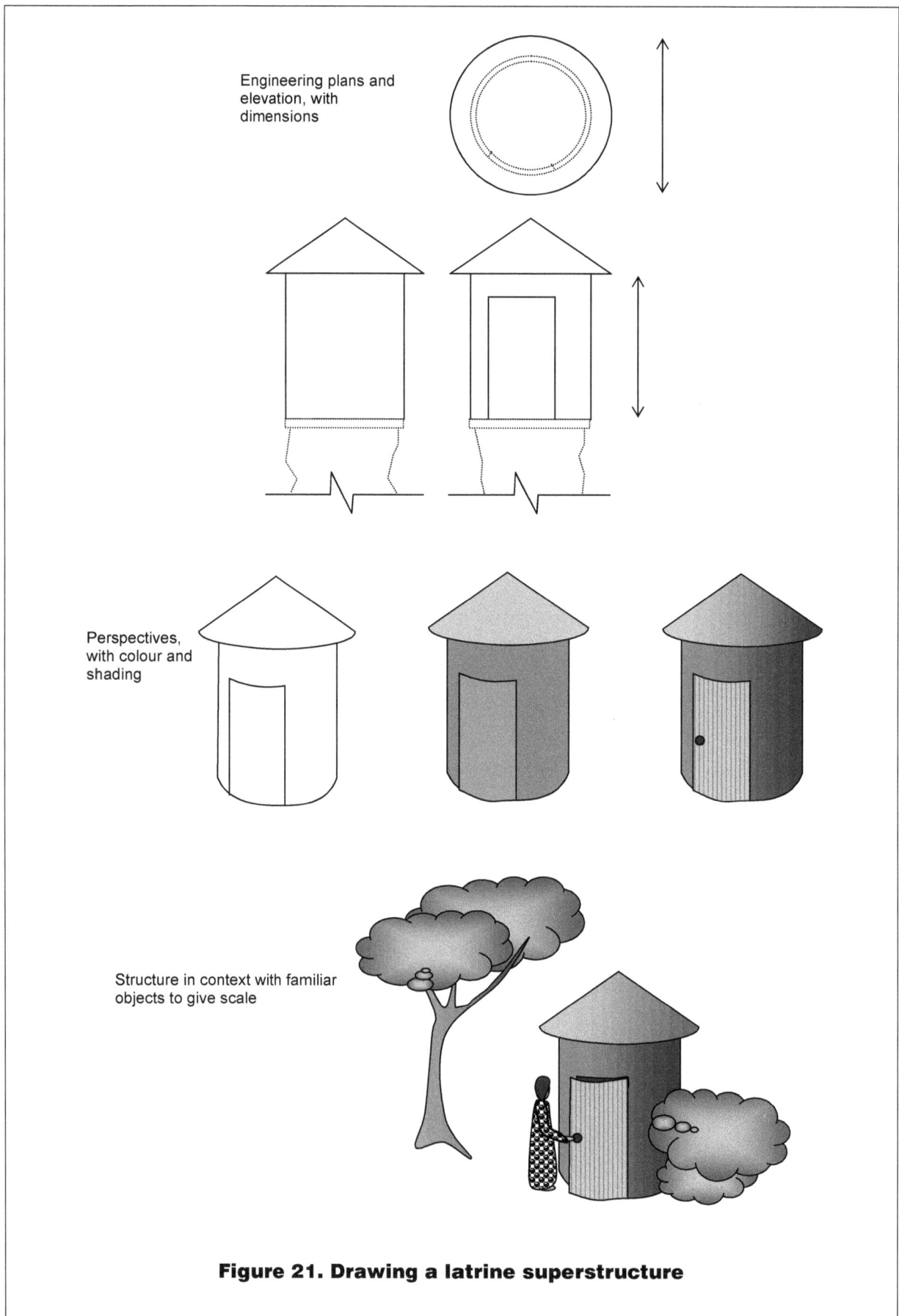

Engineering plans and elevation, with dimensions

Perspectives, with colour and shading

Structure in context with familiar objects to give scale

Figure 21. Drawing a latrine superstructure

Unit 24:
Cost/benefit analysis

Purpose

To rank the perceived cost/ benefits of a service.

Gender message

Men and women can indicate what priorities they consider important.

Engineering message

Setting priorities can involve the users, but they need to be informed about all options.

Materials

Paper or blackboard for recording lists.

Time

30 minutes

> This is also known as a *"ladder"* or *"attribute ranking"*.

In a general discussion, list the possible benefits of a service that they use (e.g. water supply, sanitation or something specific to the situation and participants, such as project vehicles). Also discuss the costs, inputs, problems of each aspect of the service, but phrase them positively. For example, maintenance is a cost, but low cost or infrequent requirement for maintenance is a benefit. Include physical issues, social impacts and perceptions.

Possible subjects include:

- Water supplies: clean water, delivery near home, easy payment system, little maintenance, convenience, reliable, reduced time

- Sanitation: health impact, privacy, convenience, cleanliness

- Irrigation: increased crop yields, reduced work in watering, reliability, convenience, reduced time.

- Project vehicles; status, speed, reliability, carrying capacity, availability, low maintenance cost

The next stage is to rank the benefits. Various methods can be used.

- Each participant can be given a set number of "points" that can be distributed amongst the options, as they feel fit. If necessary, an object such as a bean or coin could be used. Different markers could be used for men and women. If necessary, voting could be secret, or

- The group as a whole could discuss each issues and allocate up to 5 points per benefit.

Once the voting is over, put all the benefits in order. This shows what benefits the participants value the most. In a discussion, consider the costs of each of these benefits and if the order should be altered. Some benefits that are considered too costly could be moved down, whilst other issues that people would be willing to spend more on should be moved up the list.

Hints

Benefits are identified first, before costs are assigned.

Do the participants have enough knowledge to make informed choices?

Is the information they receive biased?

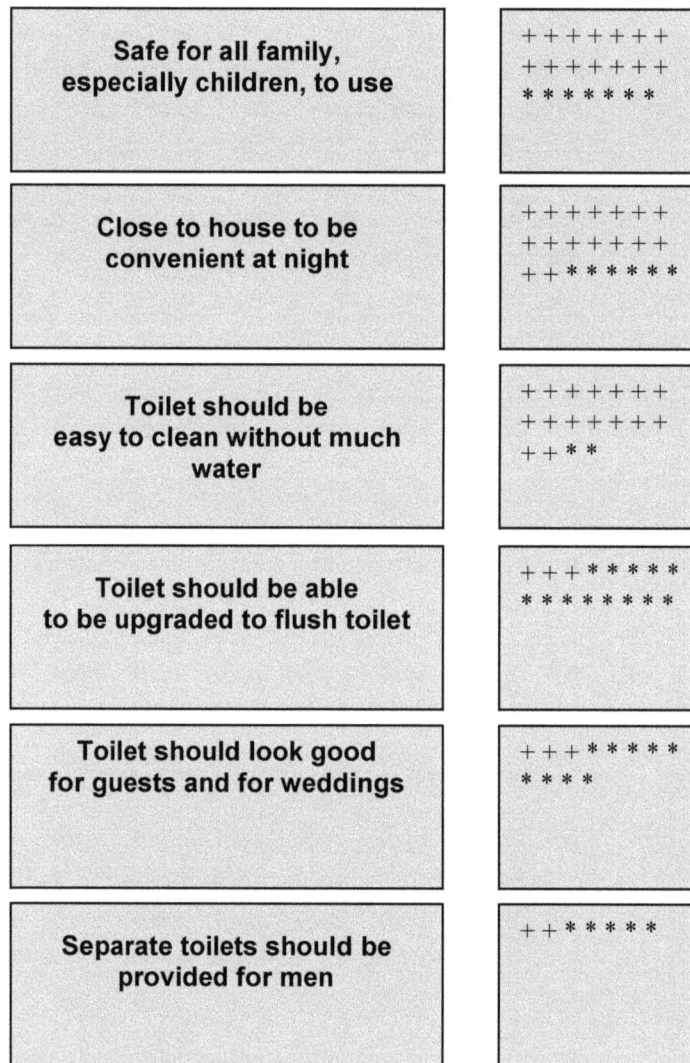

Safe for all family, especially children, to use	+ + + + + + + + + + + + * * * * * *
Close to house to be convenient at night	+ + + + + + + + + + + + + + * * * * * *
Toilet should be easy to clean without much water	+ + + + + + + + + + + + + + * *
Toilet should be able to be upgraded to flush toilet	+ + + * * * * * * * * * * * * *
Toilet should look good for guests and for weddings	+ + + * * * * * * * * *
Separate toilets should be provided for men	+ + * * * * *

The boxes on the right show the results of pocket chart voting. Each participant can place up to two markers in each box. Gender differences are revealed by using different coloured markers.

Figure 22. Example of some attribute ranking for household sanitation[9]

---

9   The example for this exercise is taken from "Designing water supply and sanitation projects to meet demand" Deverill et al. WEDC, 2002.

Unit 25:
Together or apart?

Purpose

To discuss the benefits and problems of integrating gender into infrastructure projects.

Gender message

Mainstreaming gender in engineering projects can alter both the engineering and the "gender" aspects of a project.

Engineering message

Considering "gender" allows the engineer to meet the needs of the user more closely.

Materials

Board

Time

20 minutes

> *Addressing social issues separately can make them appear different or less important than technical issues. Including them in the core of a project is sometimes called mainstreaming.*

This is a time to review what has been learnt in looking at the project process. Review:

? Who are engineering projects for (all of society)

? Who is normally excluded from discussion making (vulnerable people)

? How can vulnerable people be recognised (indicators are poor/ women/ tribal)

? How can technical staff find out what the users want (talk to them)

Copy the following diagram (either photocopy or draw on a large board). Use this a basic for discussion.

? Where on this continuum are "standard" engineering projects? (if it is near the top, you can go home!)

? Where are "best practice" projects?

? Where should we be?

This can be a general discussion. There may be good reasons not to be at the top of the scale (e.g. lack of expertise, need to have "visible" gender inputs). This will allow the facilitator to assess the level of commitment and interest from the group.

68

The users are the key to a sustainable water supply. Engineers and social scientists can facilitate the process.

Engineers and social scientists need to work together to design a water supply system

Social scientists are needed, but they can work separately from the engineers

Social issues can be sorted out once the design is complete.

There is a need, but there are issues that are more important for engineers.

If the design is correct, people can adapt to the way it works.

Water supplies require expert design and an engineer can do this.

Engineering is neutral. You do not need to consider men and women separately.

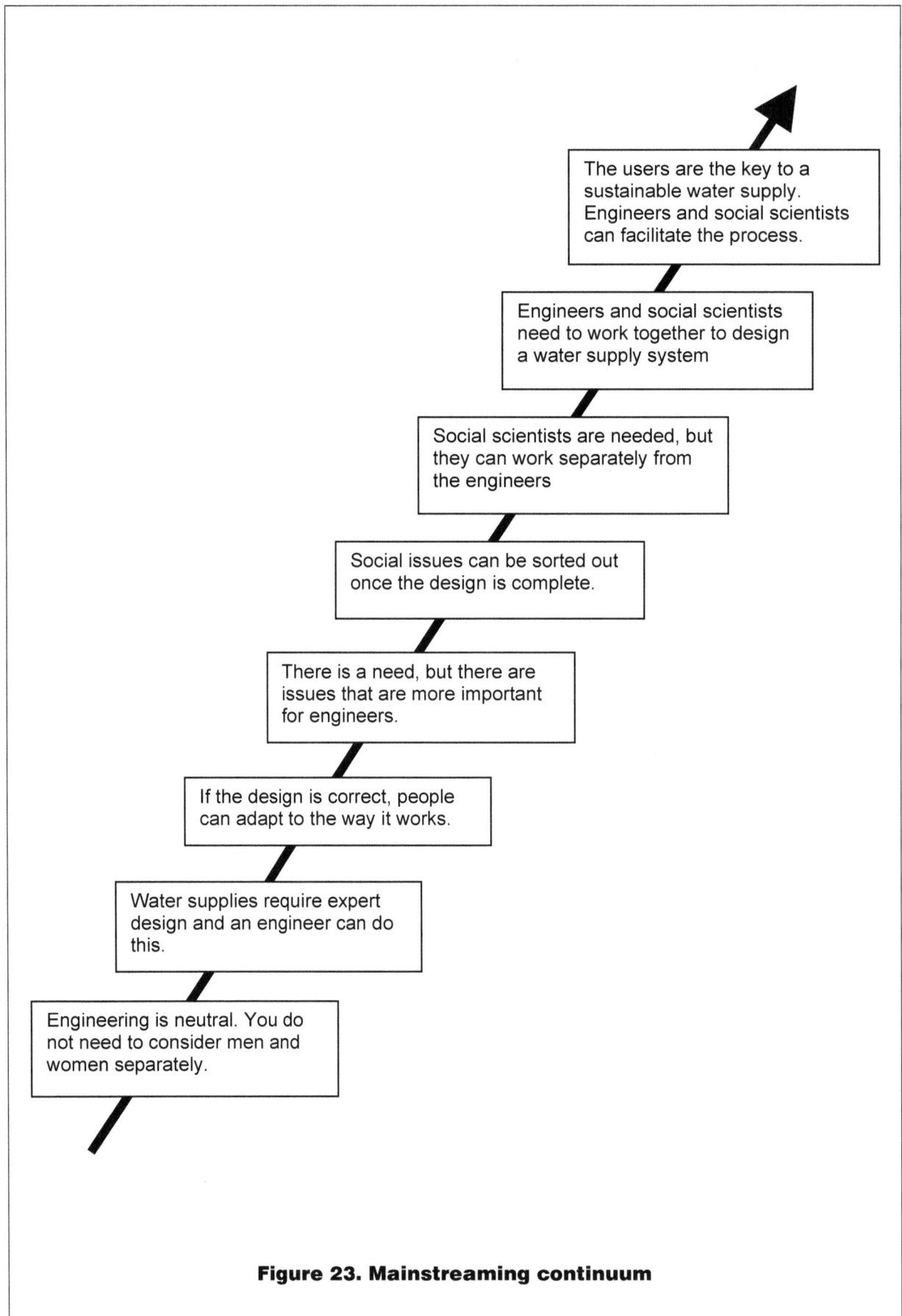

Figure 23. Mainstreaming continuum

Unit 26:
Why are we at work?

Purpose

To examine the goals of the workforce, collectively and as individuals

Gender message

Engineering organizations are not just about producing "outputs"

Engineering message

Engineering organizations are not just about producing "outputs"

Materials

None

Time

15 minutes

> *This unit is similar to the "what is civil engineering" exercise, but focussed on your organization's goals.*

In small groups, discuss what the purpose of your organization is. What are your:

- group goals

- individual goals

Are these:

- financial

- practical or

- aspirational.

If the organization has a mission statement, what is it and do people know about it?

In the full group, discuss the reasons for your organization's work. Various themes should emerge.

- The organization and the individual have financial reasons for existing (even voluntary organizations have to be financially solvent. Donations of time or money are still payments for a "service").

- The organization is not just about making money. It should be providing a service to clients.

- The service may be designs, construction or supplying materials, information or less tangible outputs.

- There may be an ethos (guiding principle) behind the organization.

- Individuals may be motivated by a variety of factors, money is only one reason why they come to work. Social factors and belief in their work may be important.

For an engineering organization, ask what resources are available to meet these goals. Normally this will be a mixture of human, physical (e.g. offices, computers, vehicles), natural (e.g. raw materials for manufacturing) and financial resources.

The discussion should identify that there are a variety of reasons for the organizations and individuals' work. These are both logical and factual (such as the need to earn a living) and to do with perceptions (e.g. working on something you enjoy or find worthwhile).

Hints

If there are several organizations amongst the group, or if people are from different departments, dividing them along these institutional lines may demonstrate differences - both real and perceived.

Unit 27:
Teamwork?

Purpose

To provide a "technical break" in the training session and to create mini-organizations.

Gender message

Teams require a diverse range of skills and perspectives.

Engineering message

Some tasks are more efficient if teams of people are involved.

Materials

Various craft materials (paper, glue, card, string) plus a prize.

Time

60 minutes

> *Some tasks can be carried out by individuals (e.g. calculating hydraulics profiles of pipes), but others need a team work approach (e.g. having a variety of specialists such as a contracts expert, a hydrogeologist and a hand pump specialist).*

Develop a simple engineering problem that can be carried out in the training area using readily available materials (e.g. transfer an egg from one area to another using elastic bands, paper, card, glue, support a weight half way between two blocks only using newspaper and string). Divide the group into teams (about four people) and give them a set time to complete the task. In the full group, ask them to prove their design works, with a prize for the winning team. Set marking criteria (such as fulfilling the task x%, use of materials (cost or weight) y% and elegance of design z%).

Discuss:

? Did you work as teams or as individuals?

? What were the benefits of working in a team and what were the problems? (e.g. specialisation and communication)

? Where particular individuals or ideas ignored? Did this make the product less effective?

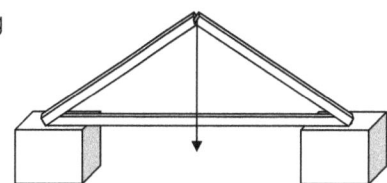

Review the issues covered in any previous sessions (such as the idea of the product and process, and involvement of all opinions). Use the unit as an introduction to discussing issues about the engineering organization.

Hints

If the teams are fairly uniform, assign roles to each member (e.g. one cannot speak unless directly ask a question, one will only speak and not carry out any practical work, one will do practical work but not speak). Each role should remain private until the end of the exercise.

Alternatively, give each person a particular interest that will be reflected in the marking schedule. Thus one person could make the design colourful, one could be concerned that one material is (or is not) used, one could insist on a particular dimension and another on a conflicting dimension. Each role should remain private until the end of the exercise, but be reflected in the marking schedule.

Unit 28:
How are we organized?

Purpose

To look the organizational structure of the workforce and its diversity.

Gender message

Human resources are an important resource for any organization. How they are managed can influence their performance.

Engineering message

Human resources are an important resource for any organization. How they are managed can influence their performance.

Materials

Paper and pens

Time

30 minutes

In small groups (perhaps from different management levels), ask each group to draw their perceptions of the organizational structure of the organization (an "organogram"). These could be compared to see if there are any variations in perception between groups. Do not forget to include all levels of staff, including support staff. Some support activities may be separated from the direct structure (e.g. cleaners in an office, specialist sub-contractors on site).

? Discuss why an organizational structure is required. Issues include:

■ specialisation (allowing expertise to develop in one area)

■ breaking work down into components

■ clear information routes

■ co-ordination of activities

? Are there any problems with having a management structure, such as:

■ vertical barriers between specialist sub-groups

■ horizontal barriers preventing information moving up or down the organization.

■ Lack of flexibility to respond to changing circumstances

Hierarchical organizational structures evolved in the government or manufacturing context, where work could be broken into small components and did not change rapidly over time.

Variations on a standard organization structure include flattened hierarchies, project and management teams and alternative group relationships such as matrix management.

? Now look at the socio-economic groups within the organization. The easiest analysis is probably gender, but there may be other factors that are more relevant. Is there a pattern?

73

Hints

This unit introduces material for other units and opens up a discussion that organizational patterns should alter to fit the task in hand.

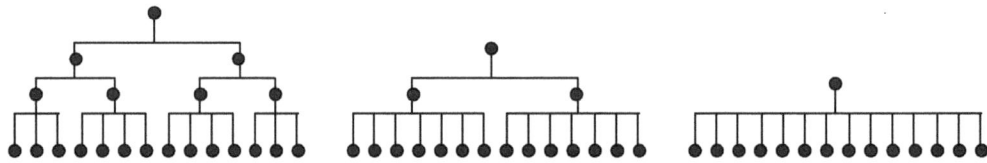

Organization with four, three and two levels of hierachy.

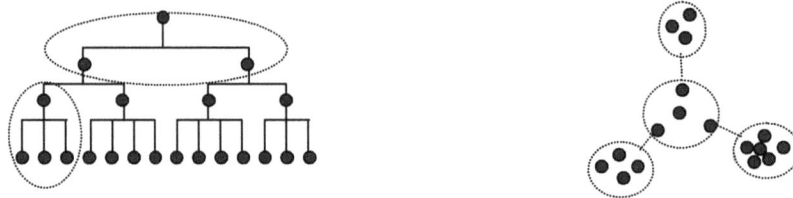

Dividing the organization into teams, with or without a hierarchy.

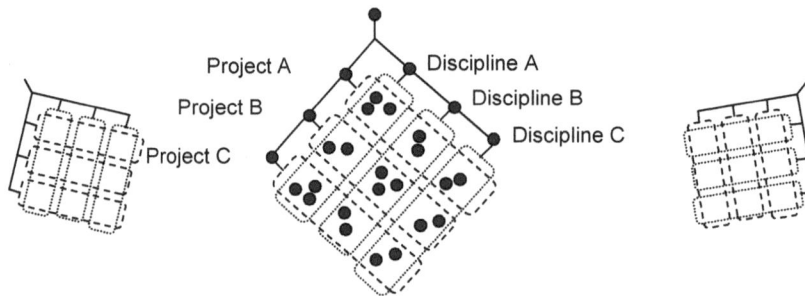

Project A   Discipline A
Project B   Discipline B
Project C   Discipline C

Matrix management – this can be discipline or project led.

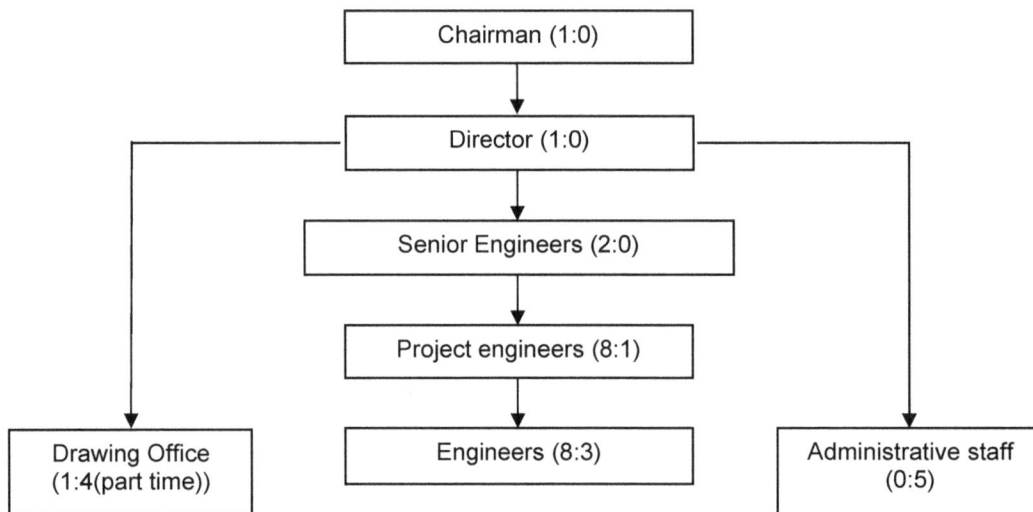

Chairman (1:0)

Director (1:0)

Senior Engineers (2:0)

Project engineers (8:1)

Drawing Office (1:4(part time))   Engineers (8:3)   Administrative staff (0:5)

Figure 24. Examples of organization diagrams

Adapted from Senior B. (2002) Organisational Change. Financial Times, Prentice Hall.

Unit 29:
Who is our potential workforce?

Purpose

To identify any disparity between the type of people working for the organization and society at large.

Gender message

Equal opportunities may not necessarily lead to numerical parity in employment.

Engineering message

Engineers can be men or women, but there may be barriers preventing some people being employed.

Materials

Paper and pens

Time

20 minutes

> *The analysis of the organization may have shown that there are disparities between the number of men and women (or some other relevant measure of diversity in society) within an organization. A common division is with women in the poorer paid, less responsible positions and men in the more powerful roles.*

Divide the participants into men and women, or some other suitable group.

? If an organization is to optimise performance, should it restrict its workforce to one social group?

? If the organization is to respect "rights", should it (consciously or unconsciously) restrict the types of people it employs?

? If there are tasks that cannot be undertaken by certain people (and why)?

? Are there skills that disadvantage may help people develop (e.g. disabled people may develop problem solving skills as they encounter practical difficulties more often than able-bodied people).

Ask each small group to present the results of their discussion in a few sentences. If time allows a longer discussion could follow, but try and ensure that the debate relates to diversity rather than becoming a male/female divide.

? Should there be 50:50 division in the workforce? In a group, list some of the positive and negative aspects of setting targets. Possible issues include:

■ having a target means that the issue is considered and progress measured.

■ data enables the workforce to be compared with similar organizations.

■ the population of possible employees is not 50:50. In engineering, only a small percentage of graduates are female, and this proportion deceases for older engineers.

■ employing people to meet targets may mean in less suitable people are engaged.

■ good people from a disadvantaged group may be seen as "token" employees, engaged for who they are, not what they can provide.

Hints

Find out what proportion of people on a local university course are female or are from other significant groups (race, class, caste).

If the discussion is too polarised along gender lines, choose a less contentious social parameter. Class, caste or disability may be suitable alternatives.

What about people already working for the organization - are we making the most of them?

Unit 30:
Unequal opportunities

Purpose

To identify reasons why some social groups are under represented in engineering.

Gender message

Barriers to equality of opportunity occur throughout somebody's career.

Engineering message

Engineers can be men or women, but there may be barriers preventing some people being employed.

Materials

Paper and pens

Time

20 minutes

Using women as an example, ask the group to identify barriers at each stage of their careers that may reduce opportunities for women to take part. This could extend all the way down to primary education. A time line comparing men and women's lives may be useful (see figure below). Other social groups may be used, based on the participants' experience (e.g. urban/rural).

Allow the groups time to compare timelines.

Ensuring that you can select workers from the whole of society, rather than restricting your choice to a smaller group, requires that recruitment practices should be open to as wide a group as possible. Discuss:

? Are applications monitored?

? Are there any barriers to specific groups (advertising, interview procedure, job description)?

Other barriers may occur before people apply for a job.

? What are they? Examples include:

- Lack of education

- Lack of a role model

- Domestic commitments

? Which of these barriers could the participants reduce?

? How long will it take for some of these initiatives to change the social pattern in engineering organizations.

Hints

If the discussion is too polarised along gender lines, choose a less contentious social parameter. Class, caste or disability may be suitable alternatives.

Sub-ordinates do not accept woman as boss.

Need a job, as a single salary is not enough to contribute to family finances

Have children, have to look after them and be able to take leave at short notice

Need own income as I cannot be dependent on my husband, especially if he dies or we divorce

Get married, husband doesn't like me working

Need own income as then I have greater rights and independence

Not allowed to work night shifts so miss out on site experience

Have problems being funded at college; have to work part-time

Girls don't study sciences

Figure 25. Examples of timelines

Female technical students from low and middle income countries[10]

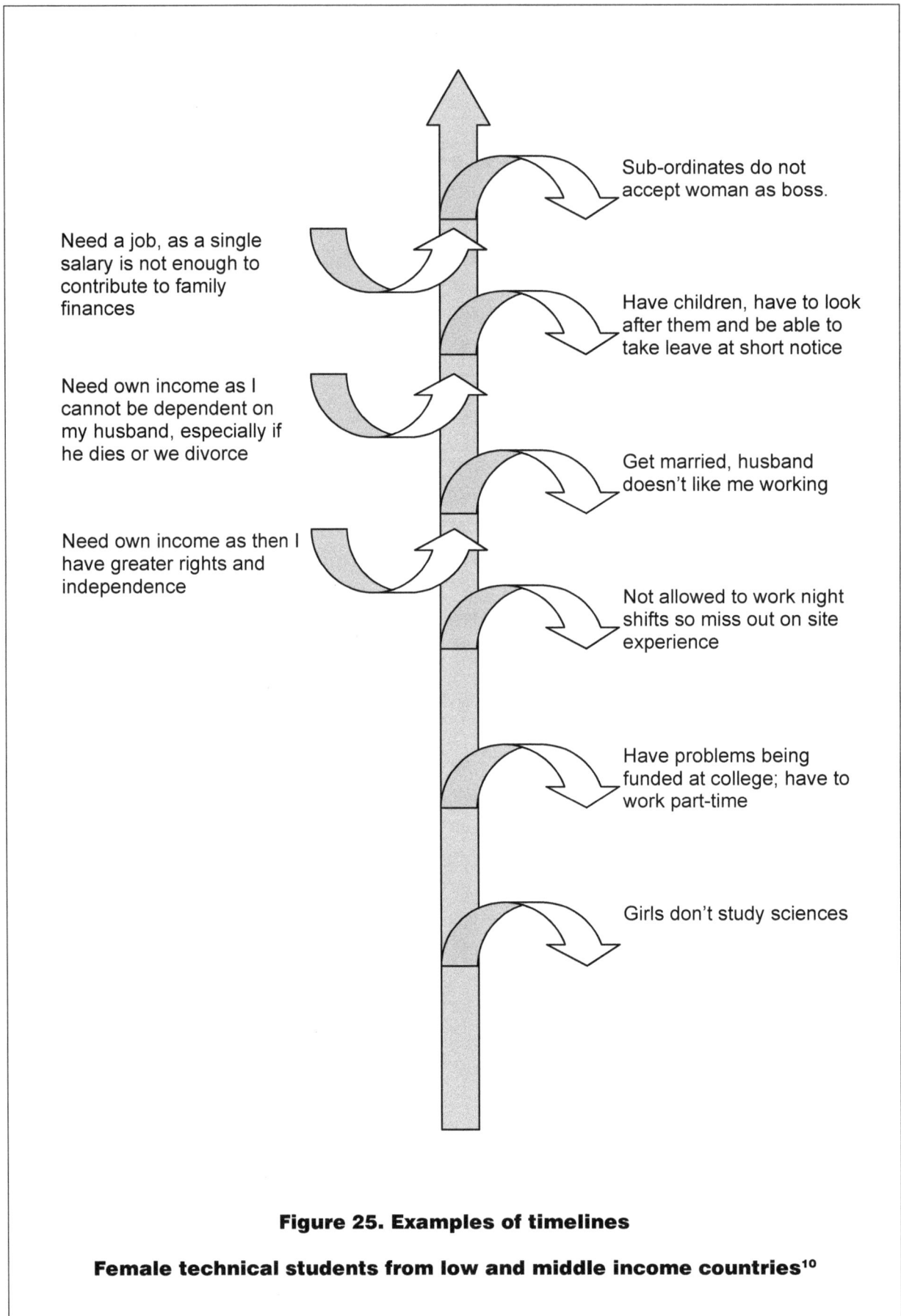

[10]   From discussions with Maria Ximena Guavita (Columbia) and Ngozi Nora Ishiekwene (Nigeria).

Colleagues competitive

A challenge – I can do this job

Need to believe in own abilities

Independent confirmation of abilities – exam results etc.

Not taken as seriously

Enabling environment – campaigns for more women in engineering

Expectations of male colleagues – can you cope in male dominated environment?

Motivated by social outcome of technical actions

In a minority at university

Parental support

Support and attitude of teachers

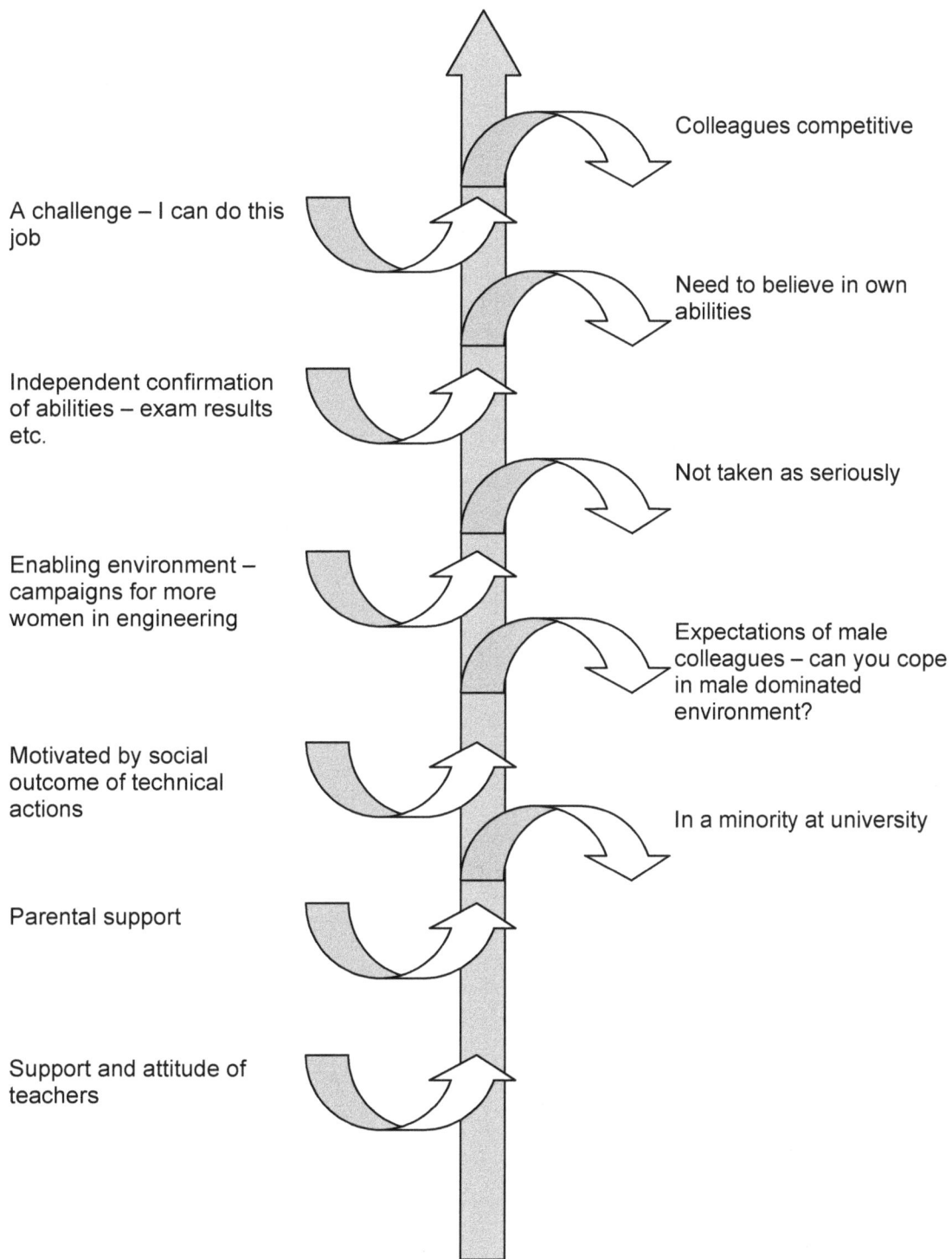

Figure 26. Examples of timelines

Female engineer – high income country[11]

---

[11]   From discussions with Rebecca Scott (UK).

Unit 31:
Life at home

Purpose

To compare the activities members of staff have to carry out at home.

Gender message

Men and women, whilst doing the same tasks at work, may have different tasks at home.

Engineering message

Domestic duties may influence work practices.

Materials

Paper and pens

Time

30 minutes

Divide the participants into small groups according to similar social groups (e.g. young single men, married women or men with children). Ask them to repeat the time chart unit (Unit 7 - What do you do with your time?), but this time ask them to record what they do either in the evening and morning outside work or activities over a weekend. Possible activities to record include:

- buying and preparing food

- cleaning the house

- looking after children

- recreational activities

- sleep

- taking children to school

Divide the activities into "domestic", "commercial", "social" and "recreational".

In the full group, compare the time charts.

? Are there differences between the social groups?

? Do these activities impact on life at work (for example childcare responsibilities, adequate rest).

? Who has to work once they get home?

Hints

If the group is solely one socio-economic group, ask participants to fill in the charts for their spouse or parents.

The culture at work and the culture at home may vary. This may be used as an alternative to a male/female comparison. E.g.;

- old people respected at home, but qualifications respected at work

- captain of a football team during recreation, sub-ordinate at work

Use these "dual lives" to demonstrate how some women have to have to juggle two lives at the same time.

Unit 32:
Practical steps

Purpose

To explore some practical changes that may increase opportunities for excluded people to work in your organization.

Gender message

Some practical actions can increase work opportunities for socially excluded people.

Engineering message

Practical actions may increase the effectiveness of all staff.

Materials

None

Time

20 minutes

> *Actions are needed to include people normally excluded from decision-making positions. Some of these can be very practical.*

Consider:

? are there suitable toilets for men/women/disabled people/ people who prefer a particular type of toilet (e.g. squat plates or pedestals)?

? is the office located so it is accessible? Consider public transport routes and personal security.

? Is the office located so people can carry out other duties on the way to work or at lunchtime (e.g. shopping, childcare)?

? does the office layout create problems (e.g. disabled access, people carrying heavy loads up stairs)?

Allow the participants time to discuss these issues. Are these issues considered by the people responsible for organising the layout of the office or by people responsible for human resources?

Other practical steps relate to working practices. Consider:

? How flexible are the working hours? Can people work part-time or work around child-care responsibilities (especially at short notice)?

? Are timetables and deadlines fixed? Could all staff work late to complete a project if necessary? Are people without "families" expected to work anti-social hours?

? Is there maternity and paternity leave?

? Is there a policy on working at home?

? What provision is made for people working in the field? Do they have to work outside normal office hours or stay overnight?

? Are staff expected to work alone in the field?

? Do allowances cover all expenses?

? Are job advertisements and recruitment procedures biased towards any particular group?

Discuss the changes and costs that some of these procedures may involve. Is the cost of employing somebody to cover paternity leave less than the cost of recruiting and training a replacement worker? Will an expectation of working anti-social hours reduce the pool of potential employees?

Hints

Some options may be a cost saving or cost neutral. Others may cost money but is a contented, stable workforce more efficient than a group of people who are always changing jobs?

Unit 33:
Breaking the glass ceiling

Purpose

To look at ways that excluded groups may be promoted or employed at higher levels.

Even if recruitment practices are open to men and women, retaining staff will require continuing opportunities for all staff. This includes working conditions and career development.

Gender message

Various actions may be required to enable excluded groups to become decision-makers.

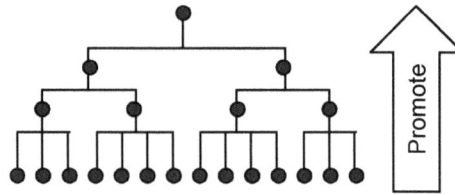

Engineering message

Career progression may depend on many factors, some explicit, some less obvious.

Discuss career paths, either within the organization or generally in the industry.

? What are the criteria for promotion?

? Do informal contacts count (e.g. social contacts such as the "old boy network" or nepotism)?

? If promotion is based on experience or responsibility, how is work assigned and responsibility delegated?

? Is work of equal value rewarded equally (e.g. do social scientists or environmentalists (often women) have the same career opportunities and pay structure as engineers?

? If additional skills or qualifications are required, are these offered equally (e.g. providing courses for engineers but not for economists)?

? Is the job description for higher grade biased for or against any social group unnecessarily?

If the group can not relate to problems women may face in career progression, consider other aspects, such as people with different social backgrounds.

Materials

None

Time

20 minutes

As with communities, there are two sides to enabling women to reach decision-making roles. Firstly, they need the skills to take up the roles. Secondly, those people who appoint decision-makers need to accept women's (or other group's) suitability and allow them to take up those roles.

Hints

Before the session, see if the organization has an equal opportunities policy or guidelines.

Unit 34:
Power to the people?

Purpose

To show there are more immediate responses to empowering excluded people.

Gender message

Gender balances can change through a variety of routes.

Engineering message

Organizational structures influence social as well as pure management issues.

Materials

None

Time

20 minutes

> *In looking at communities, two routes can be taken to enable people normally excluded to take part in decision making. A long-term action is to work to break down practical and social barriers so they can achieve power. Another option is to bring decision-making to them. In the field, this can take the form of decentralised approaches and participatory methods. Similar methods can be used in organizations.*

Improve communication

Consider a organisation chart with several levels. Communication is hampered by the number of vertical divisions between levels. Increasing communication and consultation can enable the interests of all people to be considered. This however still leaves the power in the upper levels of the organization.

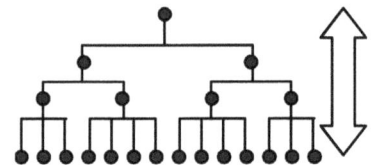

Devolve power by flattening management structures

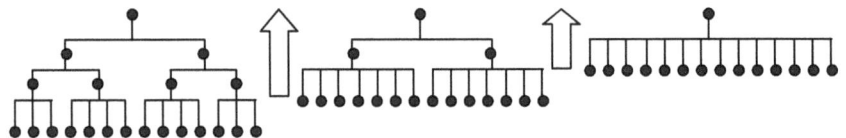

An alternative is to devolve power, through flattening the organizational hierarchy and removing levels of management.

? How flat can the structure be without confusing communication routes?

? What are the other advantages of flatter management structures? (More adaptable organizations, able to respond to changing circumstances e.g. new projects. More suitable for creative or dynamic organizations).

? What alternatives can be used that in effect flatten the management structure? (e.g. project teams, managers being a "first amongst equals" rather than being "superiors", analysing tasks - is administration the best use of an experienced person's time)

Create project teams, re-define activities or assign group representatives rather than leaders

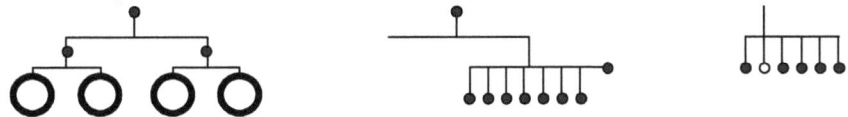

Creating smaller groups allows people who are less willing to speak out in a large group to make their voice heard. The contact point for that group could be a "first amongst equals" rather than the boss.

Hints

This unit aims to introduce ideas rather than come to any specific conclusions.

Unit 35:
Whats under the surface?

Purpose

To introduce some of the other issues (non-practical) that determine who makes decisions.

Organizations have a public face, but also action and perceptions that are behind the scenes. These factors can determine how an organization operates. This will affect both the means of improving promotion of excluded people and also increasing participation of the workforce.

Gender message

Improving opportunities does not only require practical action, but public commitment and private attitude change.

Engineering message

Organizations have formal and informal factors that determine how they operate.

Materials

Board

Time

20 minutes

On a board, draw a picture of a crocodile, hippopotamus, iceberg, boat or tree. You can see what is above the surface, but underneath there are legs, teeth, propellers, roots etc.

Explain that organizations have a public and private face. Ask the participants to write down or suggest the public view of the organization (see below for an example). Write these above the water line on your diagram.

Mission statements

Output indicators

Policies and procedures

Formal organization

Job descriptions

Input indicators

Organization charts

Informal leaders

Personal friendships

Power structures

Informal organization

Personal goals

Personal dislike

Emotions

Group norms

Informal communication

Status

Group goals

Perceptions

Now ask for issues that are not so public; again, examples are given.

? Which factors affect the opportunities open to women or other disadvantaged groups? (both public and private)

? Which factors can be changed easily? (some of the public ones)

? Who needs to act? (leaders for public issues, all staff for public and private issues)

Hints

It may be easier to post some issues anonymously, or to divide people into groups from different levels in an organization.

Unit 36:
Are we ready for change?

Purpose

To decide where the organization is in terms of inclusive work practices.

Gender message

Change takes time.

Engineering message

Change takes time.

Materials

Copy of chart.

Time

10 minutes

> Social change takes a long time. Having the will to change the physical working environment or employment conditions also requires a willingness to carry out the actions - and allocate resources to them. Including the excluded involves one group beginning to share power with others and can be threatening.
>
> Trying to introduce ideas before the organization is ready for change can frustrate both the people campaigning for change and those who do not yet accept the need for change.

If the group is large, divide into smaller groups. Using the continuum chart below, discuss:

?   Where is the organization as a whole?

?   Are different parts of the organization at different stages?

?   Where was the organization five years ago?

?   Where will it be in five years?

Decide when to revisit the chart - but do not expect change in months!

Hints

Try to get the participants to "step outside" their organization and view it dispassionately. Those in-charge need to view widening decision-making as an increase in overall strength, rather than them losing power.

This also could be used to assess the level of interest at the start of the training session.

Our organization is inclusive and decision making is open to people from all social groups

Equality of opportunity will make our organizations more effective and efficient

The managers will have to lead any change to make our organization inclusive

Working conditions can be adjusted to include more members of society

The only way for socially excluded groups to have equality is for attitudes to change in society

Some groups need the physical working environment adapted to their needs

All engineers are the same and employment and promotion is on merit not other factors

If a woman wants to be an engineer, that is OK, but she needs no special treatment

Women do not make good engineers

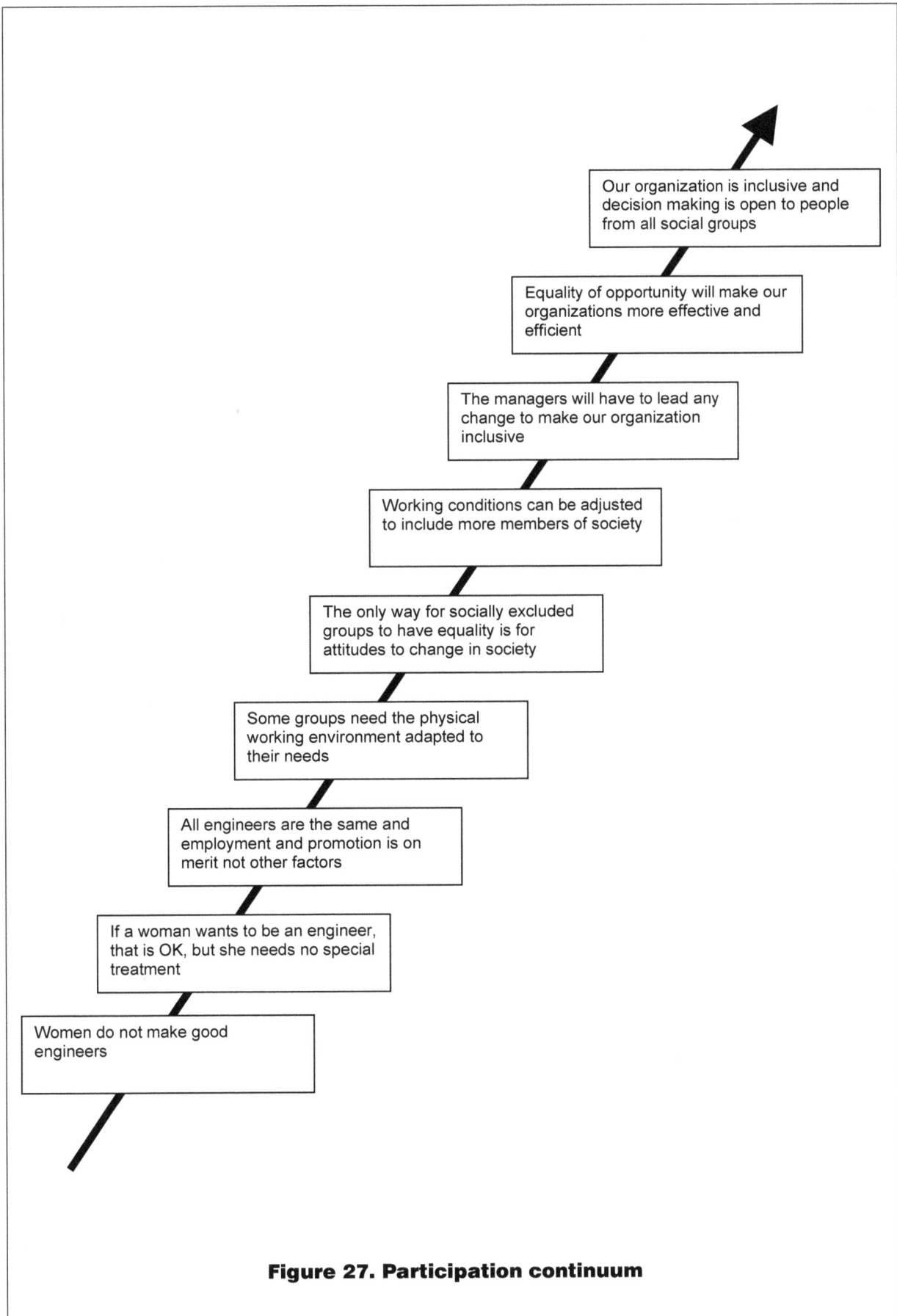

Figure 27. Participation continuum

Unit 37:
Putting gender on the agenda

Purpose

To decide what action should and could be taken to make an organization more inclusive.

Gender message

Just as projects have to be tailored to the needs of particular circumstances, there is no standard response to making organizations more inclusive.

Engineering message

You spend a large amount of time working for organizations. What do you want them to be like and how can you move in that direction?

Materials

People's minds

Time

20 years (minimum)

> *How, why and how fast an organization can make its workforce more diverse and open up decision making to a wider group will depend on the organization and what stage they are at. Any activities must be context specific and owned by all parts of the organization. Consider what your organization can do.*
>
> *If the facilitator is external, they may want to hand over the session to members of the organization.*

This unit has to be related to the organization and should be drafted once previous units have been completed.

Hints

Do not plan anything too ambitious to begin with.

Evolution may be faster and less painful than revolution

Expecting everybody to work for change is unrealistic - a task force or working group may be needed to focus activities

A task force should work at the pace of the whole organization - they should not leave everybody else behind

A task force should not only be made up of enthusiasts, but represent all shades of opinion and all levels of management.

Units from this training pack can be used to raise issues

Surveys, workshops, visits all can be used to promote evolution.

Use other opportunities (management change, new projects, other training courses).

Unit 38:
Session review

Purpose

To check what people have learnt.

Gender message

Do the participants consider gender is an issue that they need to consider in their everyday work?

Engineering message

Do the participants consider a more equitable approach to decision-making improves engineering?

Materials

Feedback form

Time

10 minutes

> *Participative exercises may be enjoyable, but the participants may not realise that they are actually gaining knowledge, skills and understanding. Trainers may assume they are when in fact they are not! Engineers and technical staff are used to learning facts and are not so used to developing awareness of concepts.*

At the end of a session, it is useful to spend some time reflecting on what has been covered.

? What did the session cover?

? What was discussed?

? What points were learnt?

? How can this be used?

? What is the engineer's role?

? What has to be done by others?

? What else is required?

If you want to assess the impact of the training session, the following feedback form can be used.

Hints

Allow individuals time to feedback.

Discuss with the group how the key messages or lessons learned may lead to impact at work, or on the project. How might this be measured? How can it be monitored? Who should be involved?

Feedback

In order to check that the participants have understood the training sessions, it is useful to ask them to comment on the training.

Feedback forms

These can be anonymous and allow the trainer to assess how the session has worked. Prepare your own forms related to your particular format. Various ways can be used to quantify each aspect. e.g.

- Excellent/good/acceptable/poor

- 5 4 3 2 1 (5 is excellent, 1 is poor)

- excellent <--------------!-----------> poor

- 100% -0%

- extremely useful/very useful/useful/not useful

The following questions can be used as a basis for a feedback form.

How the sessions were led (presentation)

Was the location appropriate?
Presenter
Presentation techniques
Timing
What the best
What could be improved

What the sessions included (content)

What was best about the session?
What could be improved?
What was missed out?
Subject matter
Relevance/usefulness
Do you feel you understand more about ... (insert purpose of session).

Any other comments?

Participative technique

An alternative method of assessing the impact of the training session is to use a ladder (see unit 24). Participants can indicate where they think they are on the scale and if they have changed.[12]

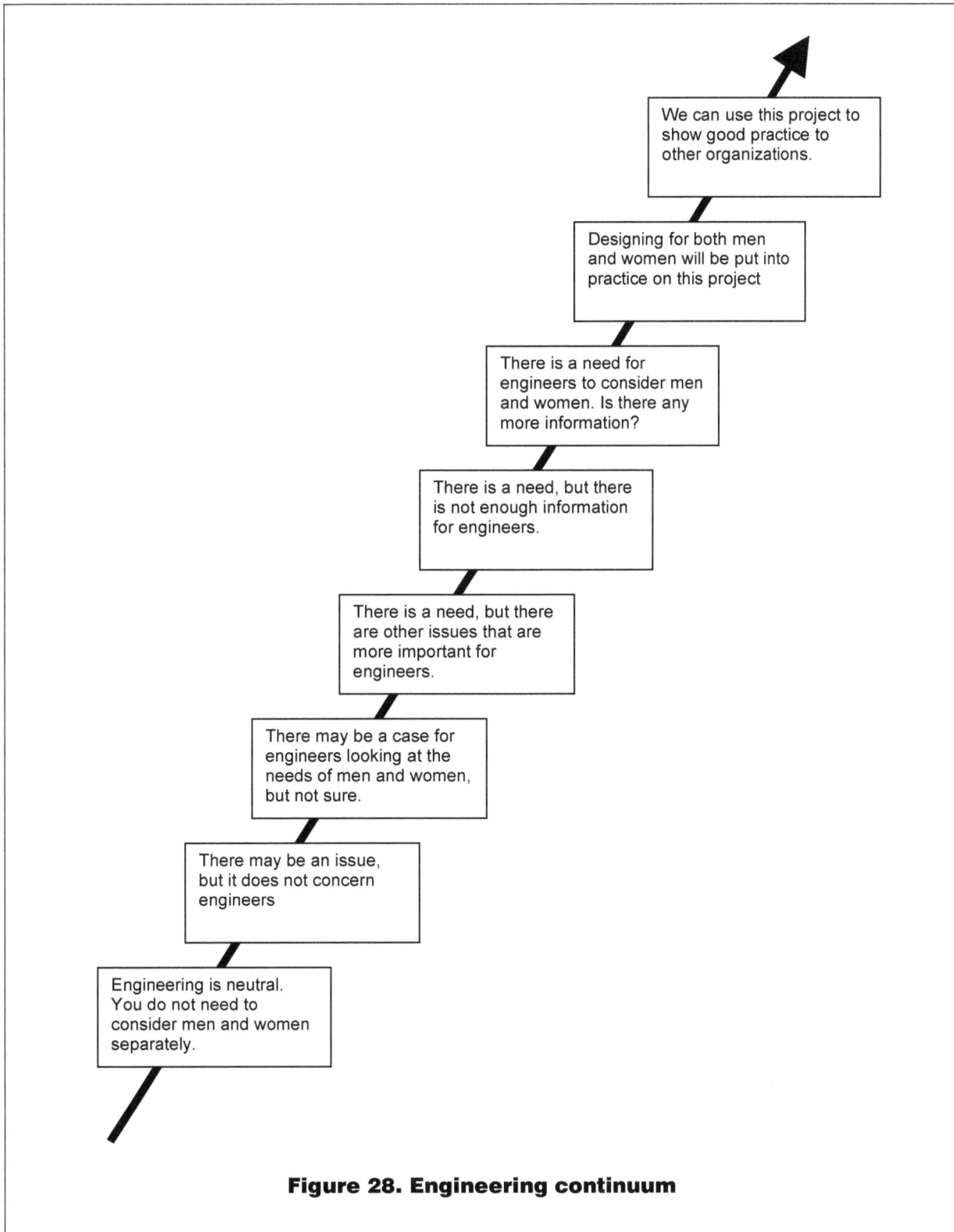

We can use this project to show good practice to other organizations.

Designing for both men and women will be put into practice on this project

There is a need for engineers to consider men and women. Is there any more information?

There is a need, but there is not enough information for engineers.

There is a need, but there are other issues that are more important for engineers.

There may be a case for engineers looking at the needs of men and women, but not sure.

There may be an issue, but it does not concern engineers

Engineering is neutral. You do not need to consider men and women separately.

Figure 28. Engineering continuum

---

[12] Based on the Change Continuum Ladder produced by UNICEF PHE project, Zimbabwe.

Checklists

These could be used at meetings, for self-assessment at different stages of the project, in preparing designs, plans or reports or as a basis for discussions with project partners and funders.

Checklist 1:
Project planning review

The following notes can be used as a checklist to ensure that issues of social exclusion are integrated into an infrastructure project from the start rather than at a later stage.

Policies

? What are the sector policies and commitments to water coverage (or sanitation or other sector) and social exclusion/ gender?

? What are the national policies and commitments to water coverage (or sanitation or other sector) and social exclusion/ gender?

? What are the international policies and commitments to water coverage (or sanitation or other sector) and social exclusion/ gender?

? Are there social aspects of the water, sanitation or irrigation policies

? Are there practical aspects of gender policies?

? Do the policies work together or conflict? e.g. does cost recovery consider female -headed households?

Practice

? What approaches are other agencies taking to gender mainstreaming in the sector?

? Does statistical data collection in the sector include appropriate disaggregation by sex, age, tribe, "wealth" or other relevant indicator of social exclusion?

? Do Terms of Reference require gender issues to be considered in all stages of the project cycle?

Capacity

? Are national and local officials in the sector sufficiently aware of gender issues? If not how can they be encouraged to mainstream gender in their work?

? Does current land, water and credit legislation in practice exclude some members of society from access to services e.g. women, the landless, poor men, and minorities? If so, what measures are in place to alter the 'status quo'?

? Are there economic, social or cultural barriers to women's participation in the planning and implementation of projects? If so what plans have been made to eliminate these barriers?

? Does the programme strategy include a planned process for building acceptance for gender equality (or other disadvantaged group)? Does this work extend beyond the community level to all operational, support and policy levels to ensure that it takes root?

? Have potential partners been identified in the development of a gender sensitive programme within the local context? Are they involved in the programming process itself?

Strategic issues

? Will the project increase the status and opportunities for women or other disadvantaged groups?

Hints

There are no correct answers to these questions. The local situation will dictate the best way forward. It is important that social exclusion is raised at an early stage, even making it one of the aims of an infrastructure project. Contradictions in policy need to be addressed before the project starts.

Look at past programmes and policies to benefit form lessons learnt.

Checklist 2:
Feasibility study meeting

? What are the rules for selecting projects? Are they clear and have they been agreed?

? Who makes the final decision?

? Who is the "client"? - The user, the manager or the funder?

? Who are the stakeholders? Do they have representative organizations?

? Have the stakeholders been consulted? - if not, when will they be involved?

? What were they consulted about - were women only asked about social and not technical options?

? Are there any barriers to consultation?

? Do you need somebody acceptable to a group who understands engineering and participation?

? Are any groups constrained from consultations due to time, resources or social restrictions?

? Do all groups have equal information about the project?

? Do all groups have equal opportunities to state their view of the issue and voice their demands?

? Do stakeholder priorities differ?

? Do all groups have equal opportunities to influence decisions?

? Is the project flexible enough to change to meet the needs of users later in the project cycle?

? What are the physical (infrastructure) and social (behaviour) changes necessary to reach the goals?

? What is the physical product of the project (if any)? Can it be used by all people?

? What are the social, economic, environmental impacts of the physical infrastructure?

   ? Who benefits? - Who pays a cost?

? What are the institutional and management results of the project? Are they open to all people?

? What are the existing power structures? Will they alter?

? What are the social, economic, environmental impacts of the way the project is to be carried out?

   ? Who benefits? - Who pays a cost?

? Will the project benefit women as well as men, poor as well as rich?

? Is support being provided to enhance the status of socially excluded groups? - both to the group directly and generally in society?

? Are baseline data on current practices and future demands disaggregated by sex wherever possible

Strategic issues

? Will the project increase the status and opportunities for women or other disadvantaged groups?

Hints

There may not be equal opportunities for all and some people will not have complete information, but this state of disparity needs to be recognised and allowed for. Bias may need to be given to disadvantaged groups.

Briefly, re-visit the policy agenda to see if policy is constraining or promoting any aspect of the project at this stage.

Checklist 3:
Project approval meeting

? What is the project purpose? Does this include a practical and strategic improvement in the position of marginalized people?

? Does the proposed project meet the project purpose?

? Are there any alternatives?

? What are the risks and assumptions? Is one stakeholder group more at risk than other people are?

? What is the long-term sustainability of the project? Who has an interest in keeping it working?

? What are the indicators to be used to measure social aspects of the project? Are these relevant to the core of the project?

Strategic issues

? Is involvement in the project increasing the status and opportunities for women or other disadvantaged groups?

Hints

Review the questions that should have been asked at the previous stages as well. This stage will commit resources (people and money) so it is an opportunity to ensure it proceeds in the correct direction and has the optimum social and physical impact.

Checklist 4:
Design meeting

Process

? What are the terms of reference/ design specification?

? Do the terms of reference include social aspects and impacts of engineering?

? Is there going to be participation?

? After consultation, do any of the policies, budgets, programmes and goals need to be revised?

? Who will make the final choice on technology, management system and finance?

? Do all stakeholders accept the participative process - including engineers and funders?

? What indicators are going to be used to measure the involvement of socially excluded groups?

Programme

? Has participation been programmed into the project so there is sufficient time?

? Has it been programmed so information from the community is available before design?

? Has it been programmed so unavailable options are ruled out before being offered?

? Has is been programmed so the community is kept aware of progress and not only consulted when the project team need information?

? Do all stakeholders accept a process approach based on milestones rather than fixed construction schedules- including engineers and funders?

Participation

? Will the participation demonstrate the different (social and physical) needs of the various groups in society?

? Will it encourage dominant groups to accept the need for others' views to be considered?

? Will it encourage the socially excluded groups to contribute?

? Will the community - or sections of the community - require engineering information to make informed choices?

? Will the community - or sections of the community - require economic and management information to make informed choices?

? Does the participation exclude anybody? Think about poor, illiterate women from minority tribal/ caste/class groups.

? Can timing, choice of project personnel, type of participation and location increase access?

? Preparation - is the community involved in collecting engineering data?

- Water sources

- Water use - domestic, commercial and community

- Cropping patterns

- Health data

- Population statistics

- Desired service levels and water consumption of different people

- Existing payment, institutions and management systems

- Ability and willingness to pay - and who will be responsible for capital and operational costs

- Construction practices - how are things built traditionally and who does the work?

? Is all this data separated by sex?

Product

? Are the physical designs suitable for men and women? Have they been asked what they want?

? Is standardisation appropriate in the context of this project? Does the selected technology meet all local demands and preferences?

? Are there any physical, economic or social barriers that prevent men or women from using the infrastructure?

? How are options being communicated to different groups?

? Are different options being offered to individuals, households or neighbourhoods as appropriate? Who makes the choice?

? Does the design suit the construction technique (e.g. poor people may be able to use masonry but concrete would require trained technicians)?

Strategic issues

? Is involvement in the project increasing the status and opportunities for women or other disadvantaged groups?

Hints

The design stage is a significant engineering activity and so you may wish to divide these questions into smaller sections. They may need to be reviewed at various stages of the design.

Checklist 5:
Construction meeting

? Are men and women willing and able to contribute to the construction of the project?

? Are they to be paid?

? Are there equal opportunities for men and women to participate in paid work (or other rewards)?

? What measure are you going to use for setting payment? Is this fair for men and women?

? How is the division of labour to be allocated?

? Who is going to supervise the work?

? Can women contribute within their daily schedule without becoming overburdened or neglecting other duties (e.g. childcare, subsistence farming, and paid employment)?

? Is there scope for training women as well as men to undertake skilled work?

? Are the proposed construction methods and equipment safe and appropriate for men and women?

? Are the social development opportunities of the construction stage being used?

? Are the people who will be maintaining the systems involved in construction?

? Is the construction programme linked to other activities (e.g. hygiene promotion, management training).

? Can the design be adjusted during construction as people see what is being built?

Strategic issues

? Is involvement in the project increasing the status and opportunities for women or other disadvantaged groups?

Hints

Discussions about the use of tools, construction methods etc. could take place on site.

Payment by piecework may not be fair. Women may be able to dig more of a trench than men can, if men are selected to work on the harder, stony sections.

Different types of work may be paid at different rates. Should people building a roof earn more than the people plastering the walls only because men work on the roof and women work on plastering?

"Voluntary" labour may result in less influential members of society doing all the work.

What are the barriers to women's involvement (lack of skills may require training, illiteracy may mean appropriate contracts have to be used, other responsibilities may necessitate part-time working).

If you are on site, ask people to pick up different sized tools e.g. a lump hammer (300mm long) and a sledgehammer (1000mm long) or a spade and a shovel. Which are more suitable for smaller people?

Checklist 6:
Operation and maintenance meeting

Management

? Who is responsible for the management of the infrastructure? Are there several layers of management?

? Are men and women represented at each level? Are they active or just making up a quota?

? Are men and women represented in each aspect of the work (e.g. finance and technical)

? Where is the main decision-making power?

? Who are the main users? Are they represented?

Maintenance

? Is the system working?

? Who is employed to carry out maintenance work

? Are there any differences between the work men and women carry out on the system? Do they equal reward for equal work?

? Are their any physical, social or economic barriers to women working? Would training, changing the management system, re-assessing the tasks or adapting the infrastructure improve opportunities?

Strategic issues

? Is involvement in the project increasing the status and opportunities for women or other disadvantaged groups?

Hints

This meeting can take place around a water-point or similar focus for the users of a service.

Checklist 7:
Evaluation meeting

Policy

? What are the policies that formed the project?

? What were the terms of reference?

? What social aspects should have been addressed?

Participation

? Were social issues, such as exclusion of vulnerable groups, included in all aspects (technical, economic, management) rather than just being regarded as a separate issue?

? Were valid stakeholder representatives involved in all stages of the project cycle? What weight was given to contributions from socially excluded groups?

? Were there resources to allow the demands of men and women to be heard and acted upon?

? Who made decisions?

? Did the funders, project staff and other stakeholders not directly using the system accept the involvement of the users?

? Is the evaluation involving all stakeholders?

Practice

? What was the initial assessment of vulnerable groups?

? Were all socially excluded groups recognised (e.g. women included but poor women excluded)?

? Did the design develop to reflect the users' needs?

? Were immediate needs met?

? Is the system working? Can everybody use the system? Is it being used as designed?

? Is there equitable access to the service? - measure number of water points or similar indicators and compare this to social divisions within the community? Do the poor have further to walk?

? How is the system being used? Have patterns of use changed from the initial situation (e.g. men collecting water, women growing commercial crops)?

? Are the users happy with the service? Compare male and female opinions.

? Have people further adapted the service to their needs?

Strategic issues

? Has the project increased the status and opportunities for women or other disadvantaged groups or is it too early to decide?

? Has it made the position worse?

? Are disadvantaged groups more able to take part in managing infrastructure?

? Has the project started other longer-term activities (income generation, social groups)?

? Are the findings of the evaluation going to be shared with the community and other professionals?

Checklist 8:
Project extension meeting

? Has policy changed since the previous project?

? Have institutions changed since the previous project?

? Has the status of women and the poor changed since the previous project?

? Are all potential users served by the previous project?

Strategic issues

? Will a new project increase the status and opportunities for women or other disadvantaged groups?

Modules:
Suggested modules

Individual units can be used by themselves or in groups to form a longer training session. These sessions could be used as single activities (e.g. introducing gender), as part of a training course on another subject (e.g. hand pump design) or as a training course, either all together or spread over time (e.g. lunchtimes or after monthly progress meetings). It is important to select the programme of delivery that suits the organization, the workload of staff and the way they prefer to learn.

| Single unit | Several units forming module | Module as part of a wider training course | Modules grouped into a training course | Modules used over time to develop staff |

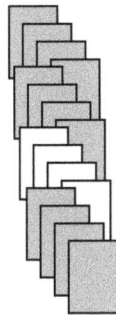

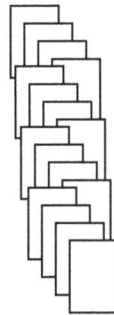

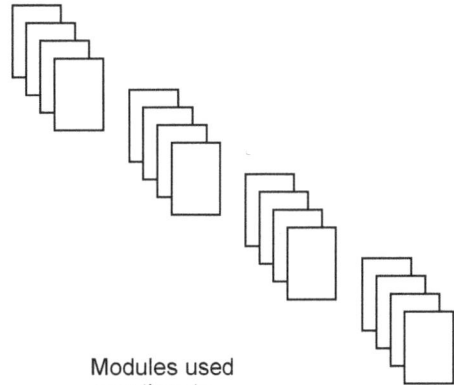

Options

Where several options are given, either a single unit can be used, or several units, either in parallel or in sequence. The first option takes the least time, but only introduces one unit. The third scenario takes longest, gives everybody an opportunity to experience the exercise, but might get repetitive. The middle scenario requires time for each exercise to be introduced to smaller groups and for their experiences to be shared at the end, but allows a variety of issues to be addressed when time is limited.

Select one unit

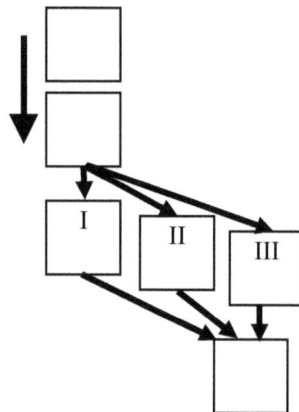

Several units in parallel

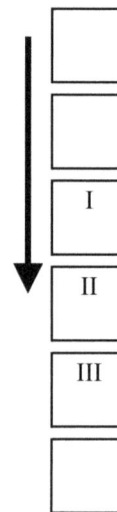

Several units in series

The following modules are only suggestions. Possible timings do not include breaks.

Module 1:
Introduction

Purpose

To raise awareness that civil engineering services are for the whole of society and different groups may have different needs.

Gender message

Men and women may have different requirements from infrastructure.

Somebody's sex is a simple indicator of his or her decision-making status in society.

Engineering message

Engineering is for the whole of society. Society is not uniform and different people may have different requirements.

Time

2-3 hours

■ Introductions (optional) - 10 minutes

■ Unit 1 - Defining civil engineering; looking at what civil engineers do and why

■ Unit 2 - Who makes up society? looking at who civil engineering is for

  – Unit 6 - Institutional analysis; looking at how society is organised (optional - just use general cases) (may be used later).

■ Unit 3 - Social exclusion; looking at who is excluded from deciding what infrastructure is provided and how it is provided and managed.

> *These units show that engineering is for people. Ignoring the needs of large segments of society makes the investment in infrastructure less efficient and effective.*

■ Either one of these, or one, two or three in series or in parallel

  – Unit 5 - Design specifications; looking at how simple design parameters can vary according to who is asked

  – Unit 21 - Designing a pit latrine slab; looking at how simple design parameters can vary according to who is asked (may be used later)

  – Unit 22 - Well wall design; looking at how simple design parameters can vary according to who is asked, (may be used later)

> *These exercises show that men and women (or other groups) may require different design details to be included in the development and management of infrastructure.*
>
> *They do not show how the opinions of the community can be ascertained.*

- Unit 4 - Social inclusion; looking at methods of including the views of excluded people the civil engineering process.

- Unit 38 - Session review (optional). Not required at this stage if part of a longer programme.

This module could be condensed to an hour, to introduce the ideas that:

- *Engineers serve society*

- *Society is varied*

- *Different people will require different outcomes from an engineering project*

- *Poor women (and children) have less influence on technical decisions than rich men.*

Module 2:
The engineering process

Purpose

To look at the engineering process and how it can miss out the needs of vulnerable groups.

Gender message

Conventional participative techniques, whilst empowering and highlighting gender as an issue, may not provide engineers with any ideas on how to change their work process.

Engineering message

Participative tools can be used to raise awareness of social exclusion and provide some analysis of gender roles

Time

2 1/2 -6 hours

- Introductions (optional) - 10 minutes

- Unit 13 - The engineering process; looking at how projects can be carried out (can be set as work to be prepared earlier).

- Unit 14 - The project cycle; looking at the stages of engineering projects

> *Engineering projects can be carried out in a variety of ways and have several stages. How can people be included in the process?*

- Either (or both)

  - Unit 12 - Designing a tap stand; looking at making a simple choice.

  - Unit 5 - Design specifications; looking at how design parameters can vary

> *People need to be included. How can we ask them what they want? Who do we ask?*

- Any/all of

  - Unit 6 - Institutional analysis; looking at who belongs to which group in society (if not used before - or repeat with based on a community).

  - Unit 7 - What do you do with your time? looking at the different ways people spend their time (parts A and/or B)

  - Unit 8 - How is the work shared out? ILooking at tasks people carry out

  - Unit 19 - Community Maps; looking at people's views of where they live

> *These units show that men and women may have different roles in society. A common method of analysis is: domestic work, commercial work and community work*

■ and either/ both *(optional)*

- Unit 10 - Whose perspective? looking at an issue from different angles.

- Unit 11 - Who knows what? looking at different levels of knowledge.

and

- Unit 9 - Census; looking at a simple way of collecting information.

> *These units generally show that participative units do not provide much technical information. However pure factual collection of information does not change people's viewpoints or raise awareness. These three sets of units can be carried out in parallel or series, depending on time and numbers of participants.*

- Unit 25 - Together or apart?

- Unit 38 - Session review (optional).

> *This module could be used without the previous module for technical staff who have some knowledge of gender or other socio-economic issues. In this case, Unit 1 - Defining civil engineering, is used as an introduction.*

Module 3:
The engineering product

Purpose

To look at the engineering product and how it can meet the needs of vulnerable groups.

Gender message

Technical issues do not affect the welfare of vulnerable groups, they can improve their status.

Engineering message

Engineers can involve people in technical decision-making.

Time

3 hours to a full day

- Introductions (optional) - 10 minutes

> *These suggestions should be adapted to suit the existing knowledge and awareness of the group. Although some engineers may be "gender aware", they may not have related it directly to engineering.*

Revisit or summarize:

- Unit 1 - Defining civil engineering; looking at what civil engineers do and why

- Unit 5 - Design specifications; looking at how design parameters can vary

Compare technical, social and management aspects of the engineered product

- Unit 18 - Faeces, fingers and food and/or

- Unit 15 - Engineering information, looking at what information is needed

> *How can data be gathered to ensure infrastructure meets people's needs?*

Either/all of:

Planning

- Unit 16 - Customer surveys, looking at "marketing" the infrastructure and/or

- Unit 17 - Problem and objective trees, helping define the issues

Data collection

- Unit 20 - Site visit, broadening the information from a standard method and/or

- Unit 9 - Census, showing the limitations of some "factual" information

Design: a choice from:

- Unit 21 - Designing a pit latrine slab and/or

- Unit 22 - Well wall design , if not used earlier

Communication

- Unit 23 - Getting the design across, and/or

- Unit 10 - Whose perspective?, as communication needs to be two way

- and either/both *(optional)*

  - Unit 10 - Whose perspective? looking at an issue from different angles.

  - Unit 11 - Who knows what? looking at different levels of knowledge.

Selection

- Unit 24 - Cost/benefit analysis

> *These units should be selected to suit the project stage, but should give an idea of what comes before and after the current stage.*

- Unit 38 - Session review *(optional)*.

Module 4:
Looking at your organisation:

Do you practice what you would like to preach?

Purpose

To look at the way the engineering organization is managed.

Gender message

A diverse workforce can improve performance, but practical and longer-term step may need to make the organization more inclusive.

Engineering message

*Gender is not just **what** is produced, or **how** it is produced, but how engineers manage their organization.*

Time

Spread over several weeks

Exercise 1 - Introductions (optional)

> *If you need to check what level of awareness your group is at, use Unit 36 - Are we ready for change? before the session starts.*

> *The units could be read as self-study material or used as a long term process over several months to develop initiatives leading to a more diverse workforce.*

- Unit 6 - Institutional analysis

- Unit 26 - Why are we at work?

- Unit 27 - Teamwork?

- Unit 28 - How are we organized?

- Unit 29 - Who is our potential workforce?

- Unit 30 - Unequal opportunities

- Unit 31 - Life at home

- Unit 32 - Practical steps

- Unit 33 - Breaking the glass ceiling

- Unit 34 - Power to the people?

- Unit 35 - What's under the surface?

- Unit 36 - Are we ready for change?

- Unit 37 - Putting gender on the agenda

and

- Unit 38 - Session review *(optional)*

This book is one of the outputs from a Knowledge and Research project funded by the Department for International Development (DFID) of the British Government.

Other outputs include:

- Building with the Community: Engineering projects to meet the needs of both men and women (WEDC, 2005)

- Infrastructure for All: Meeting the needs of both men and women in development projects – A practical guide for engineers, technicians and project managers. (WEDC, 2007)

- Case studies of relevant projects.

For further details see: http://wedc.ac.uk/publications/

www.ingramcontent.com/pod-product-compliance
Lightning Source LLC
Chambersburg PA
CBHW060957030426

42334CB00032B/3271